EDWARD WESTON

DAVID TRAVIS

EDWARD WESTON

The Last Years in Carmel

THE ART INSTITUTE OF CHICAGO │ DISTRIBUTED ART PUBLISHERS, NEW YORK

Photography and Text Credits

Photography   Ansel Adams, pages 8, 20, 42, and back cover, courtesy of
Ansel Adams Publishing Rights Trust; Imogen Cunningham, page 28, © 1978
The Imogen Cunningham Trust; Clarence John Laughlin, page 34 and fig. 12,
© The Historic New Orleans Collection; Willard Van Dyke, page 14, posthu-
mous reproduction print from original negative, © Willard Van Dyke Estate,
courtesy of Willard Van Dyke Archive, Center for Creative Photography, The
University of Arizona; Cole Weston, page 10, courtesy of Cole Weston; and
all Edward Weston photographs, © 1981 Center for Creative Photography,
Arizona Board of Regents.

Text   The quote from "The Old Stonemason" by Robinson Jeffers, from
Robinson Jeffers, *Selected Poems* (1965); and all quotes of poetry by Wallace
Stevens, from Wallace Stevens, *The Collected Poems of Wallace Stevens*, © 1954
by Wallace Stevens, are used by permission of Alfred A. Knopf, a division of
Random House, Inc.

This book was published in conjunction with the exhibition "Edward Weston:
The Last Years in Carmel," presented at The Art Institute of Chicago,
June 2–September 16, 2001; and at the San Francisco Museum of Modern Art,
March 1–July 9, 2002.

Edward Weston: The Last Years in Carmel has been organized by The Art
Institute of Chicago and supported by a major grant from American Airlines.
Additional support has been provided by Hyatt Vacation Club.

Distributed by D.A.P. / Distributed Art Publishers, 155 Sixth Avenue, 2d floor,
New York, NY 10013. Tel.: 212 627 1999;
Fax: 212 627 9484

First edition

ISBN 0–86559–192–X

Library of Congress No. 2001087121

Front cover: Edward Weston, *Point Lobos*, 1938 (detail; cat. 10).
Back cover: Ansel Adams, *Edward Weston*, 1945 (p. 42).
Frontispiece: Edward Weston, *Point Lobos*, 1944 (cat. 43).

CONTENTS

In the summer of 1938, after traveling thousands of miles through California on his second Guggenheim Fellowship, Edward Weston and Charis Wilson built a simple studio overlooking the Pacific in the scenic Carmel Highlands. It was an ideal location for a portrait photographer who had gained an international reputation for his landscapes and still lifes. Their board-and-batten shack on Wildcat Hill was only one mile south of Point Lobos, the unspoiled headland that had become the photographer's favorite site for testing ideas and finding new approaches to advance his work. Although it signaled the beginning of a new life for one of the greatest praticioners of the medium, this period of Weston's photographic activity at Point Lobos and around his home has never been thoroughly examined by itself.

A story that began so optimistically—with a new home, a new wife, and a renewed fellowship—turned, in just a few years, into

freedom. Above all he learned to use life experience as a tool of his own creativity and, more importantly, to employ it to test the truth of his results. In these terms, Weston's is an inspirational story of virtuosity, perseverance, acceptance, and fulfillment. This is the story we tell here, and is one of the glories of the history of American art, to which the masterful works of his last decade as a photographer attest.

This exhibition and catalogue appear as part of a series sponsored by American Airlines on great photographers. The American Airlines Corporate Giving Program has helped the Art Institute to bring many fine exhibitions to the city of Chicago, and this project would have remained in our vaults had it not been for their generous support. The Art Institute is also grateful for the support of Hyatt Hotels and Resorts and Hyatt Vacation Club, whose management of the historic Highlands Inn, within walking distance of

FOREWORD

something that many have seen as tragic. One might cite, as the most obvious reasons for this, the restrictions and tensions of World War II, a marriage that ended in divorce, and the onset of the artist's Parkinson's disease. From 1940 on, and certainly by 1944, many of Weston's photographs did communicate an increasingly somber mood. But if one looks beyond his photographic surfaces and subjects such as battered rocks and dead animals, one can see the emergence of a true heroic figure: Weston used his art as a way to escape from his inner turmoil and as a vessel for that turmoil.

Weston remains, however, a complex artist, one bound to more than merely the expression of emotional situations. At the same time that he was dealing with his adversities, he entered into another stage—old age—in which he placed more demands than ever before on himself as an artist and on the meanings his photographs could hold. As he addressed more profound questions of human existence, Weston, like many great artists, recognized the permanence of his own contradictions, and thus achieved a new level of judgment and

Weston's home near Carmel, has made the corporation a sensitive and natural partner in bringing these rare and powerful photographs to light. In one sense, this project began in 1959, when the McGraw family donated over two hundred Weston photographs to the museum's then fledgling collection of photography. This gift included many of the photographer's later images. The McGraws had supported Weston directly in 1953 and 1954, ensuring a lasting record of his career by helping to pay for the printing of over eight hundred of what he considered his best negatives.

Finally, I would like to acknowledge the long and deep commitment of David Travis, Curator of Photography at the Art Institute, to the work of Edward Weston. Mr. Travis's essay reveals the complexity and humanity of Weston's late work, and is offered here as a fitting tribute to this great artist's final achievement.

James N. Wood, Director and
President, The Art Institute of Chicago

Ansel Adams. *Edward Weston, Carmel Highlands, California*, 1945.

What shall I do with this absurdity—

O heart, O troubled heart—this caricature,

Decrepit age that has been tied to me

As to a dog's tail?

                        Never had I more

Excited, passionate, fantastical

Imagination, nor an ear and eye

That expected the impossible—

—WILLIAM BUTLER YEATS at the age of sixty-one, from "The Tower," 1928[1]

Cole Weston. *Edward Weston (at Point Lobos)*, 1946.

It would not have mattered if the day had been bright; it was overcast. Nor would it have mattered if Edward Weston and his youngest son, Cole, had been in Death Valley; they were on the chilly Pacific coast at Point Lobos. As Cole now tells his story of a spring day in 1946, no matter what the weather or where they were, they saw things differently. Even though the two photographers used the same kind of camera, film, developer, and paper, as Weston explained to his son, their work came from "different human beings on different levels of growth."[2]

The younger man was strong and fit, as the elder one had been before the onset of Parkinson's disease. The son could negotiate with ease the cliffs and slippery tide pools of his father's most beloved place. Cole lugged the heavy view camera and tripod over granite boulders; later, when Edward's condition worsened, Cole often had to carry him to spots difficult to reach on the magical headland that Edward claimed to know better than any man alive or dead.

I. COLE'S STORY

Beyond physique, there was a vast psychological difference between them. The twenty-seven-year-old son was still searching for his life's work. He had been a theater major in college and then trained as a photographer during World War II. Now he was his father's assistant. As a younger man, Edward too had searched for his place in the world. He had maintained a constant optimism about the future until, suddenly, his emotional universe changed. In November 1945, Edward and Charis Wilson, once his young model and muse, and later his second wife and coauthor of his many articles and books, had separated permanently. Edward's most stable and satisfying relationship with a woman had come to an end.

Cole recalls that, despite disease and divorce, Edward remained a man for whom the natural world was never dull or predictable. For Cole almost everything about Point Lobos seen through the view camera was a discovery. For Edward it was a place to judge himself against past successes and, in his new state of mind, to determine if the wind-twisted trees and ancient, surf-shaped rocks had anything more to reveal to a man who was now weathering terrible storms of his own.

As Cole relates it, the day began, as it had to, with the packing of the car with the view camera, tripod, pre-loaded film holders, and

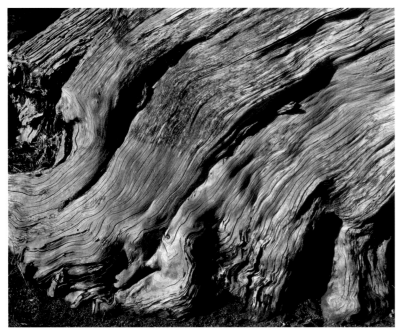

Figure 1. Edward Weston. *Cypress, Point Lobos*, 1929.

1929 was widely published, and the more spiritually resonant *China Cove, Point Lobos,* 1940 (cat. 20), was becoming a new favorite of Weston's admirers. But those were past glories, and on this particular day the two photographers were headed for the peninsula's northern shore, whose bluffs are high and steep, and for the coarse-grained, gray Santa Lucia granite rocks, the oldest of the surrounding geology.

Cole climbed with the equipment to a difficult vantage point that featured the carcass of a single, aged cypress bleached white with exposure. On a precarious round pinnacle of rock, he balanced his tripod so that its feet could hardly be moved in any direction. After some time, Cole looked down to see Edward resting on a rock below him. More time went by, and Cole asked for assistance: "After many minutes of looking through my ground glass at this composition of rocks, dead and live cypress and succulents, I called to him and suggested that he might look through the ground glass as I felt there was something there, but I was not content with the composition."[4] Edward struggled laboriously to the higher elevation, took his son's place, and studied the situation with typical reticence.

Cole's way of telling the story implies that, to anyone nearby, there would only appear to be two men fussing with an old-fashioned view camera in an environment that would seem more appropriate for the small, 35 mm. Leica, a camera originally designed by an amateur photographer and mountain climber. But there they were, braving the seasonal onshore wind, changeable light, and inconvenient boulders for some higher goal in photography than what scores of fair-weather tourist photographers seek. At a distance, the two men would have seemed to be a team intent on the making a single photograph. But that could not quite be the case. There was a difference between them after all, a difference of lifetimes.

As a beginner entering the field of landscape photography, Cole was at the rewarding stage of finding out what a big view camera could do. He was also at the exasperating stage of trying to make photographs that were not pale imitations of his father's masterpieces. Edward's vision was impossible for his son to avoid; Cole saw his father's pictures everywhere. Although Point Lobos is one of the most scenic places along a spectacular coast, Edward had earned all of his images of it. Long before, he had tamed the camera so that it became a reliable mechanism for his own particular vision. He knew exactly what to expect of the process and no longer used it for

lunch. Cole drove because Edward had never learned. Having to be driven to places, however, is not the disadvantage it may seem to those who believe that photography is the quest of a solitary eye trying to comprehend the world. View-camera photography, because of the bulky equipment involved, is often best done with two people, a photographer and an assistant. On the day of the story, assistant and photographer traded places. Edward did not set up his own camera, satisfying himself with giving Cole what advice he requested.

Point Lobos was only a short drive north, a bit over a mile. There, a spectacular landscape awaited them, one that compacted within one square mile a grove of indigenous Monterey cypress, a meadow, an abandoned whaling and canning operation, and scores of miniature coves secluded by precipitous rock cliffs. The lupine and wild iris were in bloom. The area afforded a windy home for hovering hawks and fishing cormorants, as well as a watery domain for migrating gray whales and barking California sea lions, the occupants that gave it its Spanish name, Punta de Lobos, on a Mexican map of 1823.[3]

Edward was already famous for his photographs of Point Lobos. The picture of the flamelike cypress root (fig. 1) he made in curious visual surprises. He had taught himself to "previsualize": that is, to project within his own mind exactly how a finished black-and-white print would look after seeing it at the ground glass on the back of the camera.[5] Even though this was partly what he was now teaching Cole, their discussion was centered on the composition.

Whenever he tells this story, Cole indicates in one way or another the depth of experience Edward brought to any visit to Point Lobos. His father had first seen this piece of coast over thirty years before, but only as a sightseer.[6] Then, between 1929 and 1935, when Weston had operated a one-person portrait studio in the artist colony at Carmel, he came to know the unspoiled cape intimately through his photographs. In this second experience, he produced one masterful composition after another of individual rocks, roots, branches, and washed-up kelp along the hidden beaches. This was Weston's most productive period to date, the period of his famous studio still lifes of green peppers, kale, and artichokes.

So they stood looking at the same dead tree trunk, with its remaining branches standing above the confusion of scattered rocks and a dotted cover of succulents. Edward then took charge. Keeping the camera pointed in nearly the exact direction and elevation, he changed the habitual horizontal orientation of the back of the camera to allow for a vertical view. Now the view contained a darkened, mysterious area guarded by flowering stonecrop and boulders. He studied the resulting image on the ground glass and must have sensed how the cave that was not a cave, or the womb that was not a womb, further enriched the density of objects and meaning and composed them. He then inserted an eight-by-ten-inch plate holder, withdrew the sleeve, timed an exposure, closed the holder, and took away a picture for himself (fig. 2). Generously, Cole remembers that it was all done naturally enough and with such assured deliberation that he has never felt that anything had been wrested from him. Edward too was generous, for he would later say that the photograph Cole led him to that day might have borne both their signatures.

It seems a simple story, and Cole tells it with such affection that the listener feels not only the love between father and son but also that the narrative may contain a deeper meaning. In fact there is something further to tell. As Cole reaches the end of his story, to which all the colorful details are mildly irrelevant, he relates that his father turned to him after the exposure and said that he knew his

Figure 2. Edward Weston. *North Dome, Point Lobos*, 1946 (cat. 64).

son was having difficulty because he was young. Ever supportive, Edward assured Cole that time would settle how he would come to see things photographically and otherwise. If what the younger Weston sensed in front of him turned out to be beyond his grasp, he had, in his father's eyes, demonstrated the instinct of a genuine photographer. The substance that eluded him needed an artist of longer life experience to recognize what was present in the chaotic and tortured scene, and to resolve it instantly to some inner satisfaction. This reflex toward a meaning within the moment is the one inescapable demand the medium of photography makes of those who claim to have mastered it as an art.

Willard Van Dyke. *Weston at Lobos,* 1930.

The cliffed coast of central California, with its scenic edge of continent and ocean, is not what attracted Edward Weston (1886–1958) to the small town of Carmel. Nor was it the region's mild climate, which would allow him to work out of doors for ten months of the year. Early in 1929, when Weston moved to Carmel from San Francisco, he was not known as a landscape photographer. The few landscapes that date from his boyhood in Chicago and from his honeymoon to Mount Wilson, California, were mostly incidental. Only a handful of the landscapes he took in Mexico between 1924 and 1926 did he consider to be among his best works. Weston was known for his nudes, portraits of artist friends, and compositions of objects purposely arranged as still lifes. But the prospect of finding more of these subjects is not what attracted him to Carmel, either. What he had hoped to establish in the piney artist colony on the southern edge of the Monterey Peninsula was a profitable commercial portrait business among the area's residents and summer visitors.

II. CARMEL AND POINT LOBOS

Weston was encouraged in this pursuit by the success of his close friend Johan Hagemeyer, who was making ends meet as a society photographer, dividing his time between San Francisco in the winter and Carmel in the summer.[7] Following an exhibition of his work in a tea room in Carmel, Hagemeyer realized the commercial potential of the colony for a stylish portrait photographer. He had a cottage built and, after immediate success, constructed a larger studio/home, where he photographed in the mornings and occasionally held informal art exhibitions in the afternoons. In late 1928, when Hagemeyer was planning his semiannual return to San Francisco, Weston took the Dutch photographer up on his offer to rent him his Carmel home and studio.[8]

Weston arrived in Carmel with only the hope of an income. He had been living frugally from one portrait sitting to the next in San Francisco. He was forty-two years old, long separated from his first wife, and restless. He wrote in his daybook on December 5, 1928: "Brett [Edward's second son] and I have discussed taking over Johan's [Hagemeyer] Carmel place. Both of us enthused with the idea. Foolish after the start here? Perhaps,—yet health and contentment count, and we are weary of city life, the noise, dirt, confinement. Johan did well there. I should and could."[9]

No sitters appeared in the off-season until early March, as Weston had not yet been able to find introductions to Carmel society. He had, however, received an introduction of another sort. Friends drove Edward and Brett, then sixteen, down the winding road along the high cliffs and canyons some twenty-five miles south of Carmel. Here, Weston encountered a new challenge to his picture-making ability: "The 1st of March I should write in color and capitals—I started my work again!—and in the most exciting environs,—the Big Sur. My desert rocks were much easier to work with. . . . They were physically approachable, I could walk to their base, touch them. At Big Sur, one dealt with matter from hundreds of feet to many miles distant. The way will come in time to see this marriage of ocean and rock."[10]

By socializing at concerts and accepting invitations to tea, Weston netted a few sitters, which encouraged him to believe that he had come to the right place. Nevertheless, most of the exclamation points in his daybooks were reserved for entries about what he considered his real work:

> Thursday, March 21. Point Lobos! I saw it with different eyes yesterday than those of nearly fifteen years ago. And I worked, how I worked! And I have results! And I shall go again,—and again! I did not attempt the rocks, nor any general vista: I did do the cypress! Poor abused cypress,—photographed in all their picturesqueness by tourists, "pictorialists," etched, painted and generally vilified by every self-labeled "artist." But no one has done them—to my knowledge—as I have, and will. Details, fragments of the trunk, the roots,—dazzling records, technically superb, intensely visioned. Brett and Merle Armitage exclaimed over the negatives: one "like a flame," Merle said.[11]

By mid-May, Weston had started to meet Carmel residents and was photographing Robinson Jeffers, who had become the poet most closely associated with the rough and unspoiled environment of the central California coast. Jeffers, one year younger than Weston, was near the pinnacle of his fame. His style came not from urban literary circles in the East, but rather from his own notions of the tempo and primacy of the natural world and its forces in a remote site—on the continent's end, as he phrased it. Point Lobos was the appropriate place for his austere temperament and singular, poetic voice, the place that no doubt helped him to create the swell and rhythm of his long, oceanic line:

> The water is the water, the cliff is the rock, come shocks and
>   flashes of reality. The mind
> Passes, the eye closes, the spirit is a passage;
> The beauty of things was born before eyes and sufficient to
>   itself; the heart-breaking beauty
> Will remain when there is not heart to break for it.[12]

The scarred rocks, raptorial hawks, and primeval sense of the headlands that confronted the sea were for him not picnic sites or retreats for summer inspirations, but rather cold evidence of the awesome power and beauty that had always existed in nature and would continue without the need of human observation, even by talented photographers.

Jeffers and Weston got along well. After fifty Graflex negatives taken in two sessions on overcast days along rocky Carmel Point, Weston felt he had "at least twelve, from which I could chose any one, and show with my finest portraits."[13] Things now seemed to be working out for Weston's photographic future. Other influential sitters appeared. Weston photographed, got on well with, and even sold his still-life photographs to the great muckraking journalist Lincoln Steffens and his wife, Ella Winter, who had been among the first writers to settle in the newly developed artist colony.

Along with Steffens, Arnold Genthe, a San Francisco society photographer, was part of the first wave of writers, artists, and intellectuals to buy lots and build dwellings in Carmel in the years between 1905 and 1910. Genthe, Steffens, and Jeffers (who arrived in 1914) were the kind of residents the visionary founders of the town, James Franklin Devendorf and Frank Powers, had hoped to attract, as the two enlightened businessmen had not wanted to create yet another enclave of wealthy estate owners. Their first promotion in 1903 was addressed to "the School Teachers of California and other Brain Workers at Indoor Employment."[14] Within a few years, an improving economy allowed a good number of professors from Stanford University and the University of California, Berkeley, to begin building weekend and summer cottages.

In designing a bungalow with a huge living room in which he could also work, Genthe was following the lead of George Sterling, the Bay Area's most popular and colorful poet. Both were members of San Francisco's famous Bohemian Club and among the gatherers at Coppa's restaurant. Genthe described this group as "fostering talent and putting care to rout with conviviality."[15] They wanted the colony not to become another haven for stuffy society types, but rather a place to pursue their literary and artistic vocations in a natural setting. They kept their minds animated by assembling their own witty company for drinking and weekend parties on the beach, grilling steaks of freshly harvested abalone.

Among others whom Sterling attracted to Carmel was Jack London, who came as his guest at various times to work on his novels. The journalist James Hopper and poet William Rose Benét also resided in Carmel for an extended time, as did the novelist Mary Austin, who, unable to afford the expense of building her own house, rented a cottage. She took advantage of the climate by building what she called a "wick-i-up," an open, outdoor writing platform one story off the ground in the trees.

Among other literary figures who flourished in Carmel were members of Charis Wilson's family. Her grandmother, Grace MacGowan Cooke, and her great aunt, Alice MacGowan, both writers with a national following, arrived in 1908. They preceded Upton Sinclair, whose utopian colony at Helicon Hall, New Jersey, of which they had been a part, had been destroyed by fire. Charis Wilson's father, Harry Leon Wilson, arrived in 1910. As she later recalled, "At forty-three, he was older than most of the other local writers and far more commercially successful. . . . A play he had written with Booth Tarkington, *The Man From Home*, was a long-running Broadway hit that earned him the then fabulous sum of $200 a week."[16]

At the age of forty-five, Wilson married Grace MacGowan Cooke's sixteen-year-old daughter Helen, whose beauty had also attracted the attention of Sinclair Lewis (briefly a resident in Carmel), Benét, and Genthe, the latter having photographed her among the rocks in a flowing Grecian gown. They moved into a twelve-room redwood house that Wilson had built in the Carmel Highlands. This residence, called Ocean Home, was isolated on eight acres of land next to Wildcat Creek overlooking the Pacific,

five miles south of Carmel. Jeffers's wife, Una, remembered them from a dinner hosted by the Hoppers: "The Wilsons are the Harry Leon Wilsons—you know his magazine stories. They have a big place down the coast—a chef, gardeners, chauffeurs, outdoor swimming pool and that kind of thing. Mrs. W. is stunning—to look at—stunning *interesting* clothes."[17]

By the time Weston arrived in Carmel, life there was changing and threatening to change further. The city attorney had drafted an ordinance meant to stem the tide of commercialism endangering the growing community. "The City of Carmel-by-the-Sea is hereby determined to be . . . predominantly a residential city wherein business and commerce . . . are subordinated to its residential character."[18] Carmel was no longer the tiny village of three hundred that Jeffers had entered by horse-drawn coach. It now attracted more tourists, many of whom arrived by automobile. Even Jeffers's stone house, with its adjacent tower, once remote on the windswept coastline of Carmel Point, was easily accessible and, to his chagrin, becoming a landmark itself.

Many of those who had established the colony's lasting literary character were gone by the late 1920s. Some, however, stayed on. The Wilsons remained, but divorced. In 1929 Harry returned to Ocean Home after time away in Oregon. Helen was in Carmel supervising her real-estate concerns. Steffens and Jeffers had become permanent fixtures. Ella Winter organized social functions and Una Jeffers private dinners that attracted not only local talents but also such visitors as Charlie Chaplin, George Gershwin, Martha Graham, Langston Hughes, Charles Lindbergh, Dorothy Parker, Carl Sandburg, Edna St. Vincent Millay, Gertrude Stein, and John Steinbeck. Had Weston wanted to devote himself to becoming a sought-after society portraitist like Genthe (who had since moved to New York and greater fame), he could have aggressively pursued contacts easily made through Jeffers and Steffens. But Hagemeyer remembered in a 1956 interview that the reserved Weston was not an eager provider of society's essential services, and had determined a course of his own to pioneer.[19]

The more he matured, the less Weston wanted to alter his photographs to fit a vision his sitters held of themselves, and the more he came to believe that the medium was supposed to record things as they were actually seen. For nudes and still lifes, this atti-

Figure 3. Edward Weston. *Cypress, Rock, Stonecrop*, 1930.

Figure 4. Anonymous. Postcard of Point Lobos, Monterey Co., California, 1930/40.

tude did not have the same consequences it had for the vanity of his portrait clientele. To make his living, Weston would have preferred to sell what he considered his "real work"; but even with Steffens's enthusiasm, a few faithful patrons, and affluent acquaintances in Carmel buying individual photographs, it would not have been profitable enough. Living simply and sparsely, Weston now used what income he garnered from portraiture to support his nudes, still lifes, and landscapes such as those he had begun on Point Lobos, just a few miles across Carmel Bay.

Steffens purchased a print of the 1929 photograph of the cypress root that looks like a flame on first viewing (fig. 1). Even

though it eventually became one of Weston's most famous photographs of Point Lobos, it shows nothing of the landscape itself. Almost all of the photographs he took then on Point Lobos depict objects that could be found elsewhere along the coast. When he did picture something unique to Point Lobos, it was still presented as a vignette of the larger landscape (see fig. 3). The sculptural and organic geometry he discovered in objects and details is what separated his work from that of those exploiting other aspects of the scenery. The thundering surf, the particular moods of the atmosphere of salt spray or fog, cypress dramatically clinging to the cliffs, jagged silhouettes of rocks, and the distance of the horizon at sunset were elements that, for the moment, Weston left to amateurs and postcard photographers to record in clichéd compositions (see fig. 4). Weston had his own ways, his own motifs, his own standards, and his own pace at which his works evolved. For him this period was a time for introductions.

The trees were a good place to start acquainting oneself with Point Lobos, for the distinctive Monterey cypress is indigenous only to that promontory and to Cypress Point, north across the bay.[20] Fossil remains of the cones of this tree indicate that they had been abundant along the coast over eight thousand years ago. A drier climate after that time eventually killed all but those growing on the two westerly points. The rainy winters of the region provide adequate water for that season, but in the summer, when the rains cease, water comes only from condensed fog that drops to the ground from needles and the fibrous lichens hanging from the trees' branches.

The summer fogs also occur in a way particular to the area. When the southbound surface current of the ocean is deflected off-shore by geography and fluid dynamics, the cold, deep waters of the great Monterey and Carmel submarine canyons well up to the shore.[21] The frigid waters and warm summer air produce fog regularly enough to allow these trees to survive on outcrops, the wettest areas closest to the sea. The position that exposes them to fog also subjects them to the gales of winter storms from the south and the fresh breezes of spring from the northwest. Storms break the horizontal branches and shoots erratically, and steady onshore winds stream them back and create their fantastic shapes.

Weston also photographed the forms of eroded rocks at Point Lobos in his first years there. He treated them as individual elements centered in tightly crafted compositions. For Weston the trees and rocks at Point Lobos were not distant objects, but ones he could actually touch, like the boulders in the Mojave Desert that he discovered one year before. This approach of using objects he could control was similar to the way he had made his famous close-up still lifes of nautilus shells two years earlier, and to how he was now arranging vegetables in his studio to reveal their sculptural forms (see fig. 10).

The rocks were a good way to learn about the natural history of the amazing shoreline, which was currently receiving closer scientific inspection, albeit not always aesthetically informed. One contemporary California State Park Commission study on the peninsula's wildlife contains a statement that Weston would have found laughable: "Point Lobos, topographically, is varied, even though it is without any extraordinary features of landscape."[22] The mix of rock types that fascinated Weston bore little relationship to those of the larger region inland, creating a vexing problem for geologists. It was only in the mid-1960s that the theory of plate tectonics made the region as fascinating a place for geologists to test their ideas as for photographers to test their eyes and film. The uniqueness and value of the nearly pristine cape was eventually recognized officially. In 1933 the State of California, with the assistance of the Save-the-Redwoods League, purchased 348 acres

of Point Lobos for a reserve from Alexander M. Allan.[23] Allan and his wife, Satie, donated another fifteen acres of choice headlands containing the remarkable Cypress Grove to complete the reserve.[24]

When Weston first photographed at Point Lobos, the abalone cannery Allan ran had just closed, and remnants of a former whaling operation and traces of the chute for loading coal were still in evidence along a portion of the northeastern shore.[25] The whole peninsula was Allan's private property, which he kept tourists and automobile traffic from ruining by charging a modest toll. The Park Commission study had people like Weston and the then small contingent of naturalists in mind when it recommended "visits by persons who come to learn by first-hand experience something of the realities of nature. This is the most valuable use, but these persons will remain so few in number as to require no special regulations restricting their movements on foot anywhere in the park." It suggested, however, that automobiles be restricted to paved roadways and sightseers to marked trails, as the whole coast was becoming more popular every year and could as easily be overrun by thoughtless tourists as by profit-minded businessmen or real-estate developers.[26]

For Jeffers and Weston, Point Lobos was an extraordinary landscape long before zoologists and geologists were able to explain it in their own terms. Prior to its becoming a successful test case for visionary environmentalists, the peninsula was an early proving ground for these two men, who were experimenting with changing notions of poetic and photographic meaning. From the inhuman beauty of the coast, Jeffers came to posit nothing less than a personal conception of God. Weston created his own world of parallel forms, and in his later career discovered a realm beyond formalism, a new range of human moods that his photographs would capture in the coastal atmosphere, dramatic cypress trees, and weather-beaten granite.

After two years of living in Carmel next to this inspiring point of land, Weston seemed happy and settled. On March 10, 1931, he wrote in his daybook: "Is this sojourn in Carmel an attempt to escape, a refusal? Not at all! I have one clear way to give, to justify myself as a part of this whole,—through my work. Here in Carmel I can work, and from here I send out the best of my life, focused onto a few sheets of silvered paper."[27]

Ansel Adams. *Edward and Charis, Wildcat Hill*, 1939.

What brought Weston from San Francisco to Carmel in 1929—the promise of an income—also forced him to leave six years later, not knowing whether he would ever return. One could speculate that Weston was just restless again. Three years after his arrival, he wrote in his daybook, "I do doubt my ability to remain for long in one place. The very nature of my work, requiring fresh fields to conquer."[28] The Great Depression decided matters for him. In January 1935, due to lack of sitters, Weston took down his sign, "EDWARD WESTON, PHOTOGRAPHER, UNRETOUCHED PORTRAITS/PRINTS FOR COLLECTORS."[29]

Weston had offered smaller, unretouched, and less expensive prints during the hard times that ensued with the crash on Wall Street. The change had not saved his business; he wondered if it had hurt it.[30] By June, even though, or perhaps because, he had begun a passionate love affair with the young Charis Wilson in a small town where her family was well known, Weston moved to a bungalow in

III. FREEDOM AND A HOME

Santa Monica Canyon, on Mesa Road just north of Los Angeles. The portrait business he established there with his son Brett did not depend on tourists, but on old friendships and connections. Edward's most devoted patron, art director and publishing entrepreneur Merle Armitage, ever mindful of Weston's needs, gave the photographer a job in the Federal Art Project under his direction in Los Angeles, as he had already done for Edward's oldest sons, Chandler and Brett.[31]

Typically optimistic during uncertain times, Weston had written a note accompanying a Valentine's Day photograph he sent to Charis: "Come on down. If we are going to starve, we might as well do it together."[32] After seeing her mother off to Washington, D.C. to be remarried and closing the dress shop Helen had been managing in a building she owned, Charis, now, at twenty-one legally an adult, went to live with Edward (age fifty) and Brett (age twenty-four) in August 1935. Soon, they were joined by the only two Weston sons younger than she, Neil (nineteen) and Cole (sixteen), who slept on a box spring out in the garage.

Feeling trapped in his Carmel studio, Weston had dreamed of being an "adventurer on a voyage of discovery, ready to receive fresh impressions, eager for fresh horizons . . . to identify myself in, and unify with, whatever I am able to recognize as significantly part

Figure 5. Edward Weston. *Dante's View, Death Valley*, 1938.

Figure 6. Edward Weston. *Surf, Point Lobos*, 1938.

of me: the 'me' of universal rhythms."[33] A year after moving to Mesa Road, he would be living his dream every day. Supported by two Guggenheim Fellowships (awarded in 1937 and 1938), and commissions from *Westways* magazine, he would travel nearly twenty-five thousand miles with Charis by car through California, exposing over one thousand five hundred negatives. He would come to call these the "two most prolific years of my photographic life."[34]

In the bungalow on Mesa Road and on the Guggenheim trek, Weston was no longer waiting for sitters to drop by, nor was he rising alone early in the morning to write in his daybooks. That time was now gladly given over to Charis. The passionate and self-reflective diary ended with the entry dated April 20, 1934, two days before he met Charis. It seems that he had reached a point in his life in which searching for his own identity did not require a diary of self-inspection, but rather the hard work of creating new photographs one after another.[35] True as that may be, the private thoughts of an artist at the peak of his talents and entering old age, although not as conventionally romantic or vivacious as the wanderlust expressions of a searching and younger man, are perhaps more valuable for understanding the meaning and feeling that later,

deeper works contain. Charis became the writer of the two. She saw her developing talent as a vital element in their partnership, as she recorded their Guggenheim travels with literary grace and accuracy.

Because of the Guggenheim Fellowships, this period was substantially different than his former years of struggling to find time for his own work, of anxiety-ridden thoughts, and spare-time photography. It was, rather, a period of busy days devoted to the welcome labor of view-camera photography. It tested Weston's abilities, as well as a pet theory of his. As he explained:

> Photography has long been considered a mass-production medium from the standpoint of unlimited duplication of prints. But that is a factory job, requiring standardization and mechanicalization beyond the scope of the individual who uses photography as a creative expression. Not the mass-production of duplication, but the possibility of "mass-production" of original work, is, I have long felt, one of photography's most important potentialities for the artist.[36]

Although Cole accompanied Edward and Charis on their first Guggenheim trip, most of Weston's forays were with Charis alone, as the fellowship had become for them a joint project of photographer and writer. Occasionally, another son might serve as assistant, or a protégé like Willard Van Dyke might act as driver. With such companions (Charis was twenty-three; Cole, eighteen; Van Dyke, thirty-two), the fifty-two-year-old Weston felt young again. He was in fact healthy and fit and liked to prove it by outperforming his sons in various athletic challenges they staged. In addition he was abundantly confident in his chosen medium.

Although he would acquire new skills and ways of making photographs during his travels, Weston proved himself the master of two highly visual aspects of photographic picture-making. The first, precise tonal rendition, was central to his appreciation of the medium. Through it he perfected a sensibility for the subtlety of light. The second, the representation of forms that suggest similarities in subjects vastly different in scale, was a refined compositional device that he developed from his fascination with abstract shapes. These two skills resulted in a virtuosity that led him to attempt new kinds of photographs, such as the ones he took from Dante's View in Death Valley (see fig. 5). There, an immense vista, stretching for miles into the distance, appeared to him in certain exposures to be both an array of tones and an arrangement that was not unlike a close-up pattern of waves or tide marks on a beach (see fig. 6). He also encountered entirely new subjects, photographing a rainbow (in black and white), and dealt with other subjects on a daily basis, such as distant weather, spacious skies with clouds, whole trees and mountains, abandoned structures and machinery, and even a corpse, most of which required fresh ways of envisioning them as photographs.

After three-years' absence, Edward and Charis returned to the Carmel area. As she related in *California and the West*, the 1940 book about their Guggenheim Fellowship travel:

> At first it seemed we could never settle down, there was so much of California yet to see. Edward would need a darkroom of his own for printing, and we might combine traveling and photographing with hunting for a nice old house that we could buy with the Guggenheim rent budget plus the renewed *Westways* contract. It goes without saying that such a course would have produced many more negatives than possible houses, but at this point the problem was settled for us by a letter from my father: "I have a good piece of ground

going to waste across the canyon; why not come up here and build your own house?"[37]

Although Edward and Charis could have established themselves in Los Angeles, which offered Weston good potential for portrait commissions and access to Chandler's small darkroom, there was a compelling reason for choosing Carmel: Charis's aging father was ill and needed her care.

Despite his solid income, Harry Leon Wilson's finances were in trouble. The bank to which he had mortgaged Ocean Home for his brother's ill-fated prune ranch was foreclosing. He had been swindled out of some valuable stock. In addition he had become disgusted with the childishness of Hollywood and left his lucrative job advising producers who were making his stories into films. Wilson deeded 1.8 acres to his daughter and Weston, which they were able to buy from the bank at the end of the following year, after they married.[38]

Even before the purchase was assured, Edward and Charis did not envision the house they were to build as a place to impress art-colony society or clients, as was the residence Genthe had designed, some thirty years before, with its thirty-by-sixty-foot living room beamed with solid redwood timbers and supported by four large redwood trunks.[39] Rather, their home/studio was shaped by economy: the economy of their meager income and Edward's sparse and exacting lifestyle.

Edward's third son, Neil, just twenty-one in the spring of 1938, took on the job of "architect, contractor, plumber, electrician, master carpenter, and bargain hunter for materials."[40] The unpainted, pine-board structure he built had one large room of about twenty by twenty-eight feet, a pitched roof with open rafters, a fireplace for heating at one end, and two enclosed rooms at the other for a darkroom and bathroom. A kitchen counter, sink, and stove were in one corner and a bed at the far end of the room. A skylight and full-length French doors near the center faced the Pacific over an open area high enough above the Coast Road to leave them hidden from motorists (see fig. 7).[41] In addition to the main structure, he constructed an outbuilding slightly up the hill; intended as a garage, it would become Charis's study and an occasional guestroom. Another outbuilding was then put up as a garage and tool shed.

In August the house was finished enough to invite friends. Among the first visitors were the wealthy, avant-garde art collectors Walter and Lou Arensberg, whom Edward and Charis each knew independently. Charis remembered a fury of cleaning and finishing before they arrived. Walter Arensberg, she recalled, "looking around the room in his owlish way . . . announced, 'This is a palatial shack.'"[42]

If the shack was shaped by economy, it was perfectly conceived. It had everything Edward needed and nothing more. Its purpose was uncompromised by normal domestic clutter. It shared the simple, unpretentious qualities that sixteenth-century Japanese tea masters came to admire in their construction of even smaller, unadorned structures that imitated rustic farmhouses. Weston's shack possessed what the Japanese call *wabi*, which can be translated as quiet simplicity, humility, or even frugality. Had he known about them, Weston would have admired another trait of the tea masters: the elimination of inessentials, as suggested in the beginning of a poem by the greatest of them, Sen-no-Rikyu:

> *If you have one pot*
> *And can make your tea in it*
> *That will do quite well.*
> *How much does he lack himself*
> *Who must have a lot of things.*[43]

In his work and lifestyle, Weston too pared everything down to its essentials. In taking photographs, he used only a few, basic cameras, several lenses of different focal lengths, and fewer filters. His darkroom was set up for printing contact prints only, using a simple frosted light bulb suspended above the countertop. He mounted his prints on plain mats and exhibited his work without decorative overmats, even mounting them on occasion unglazed or behind single pieces of glass secured by "L" screws. In his personal habits, he ate mostly vegetarian foods that could be prepared easily and quickly. He eventually gave up smoking. He avoided medicines, preferring to fast when ill. He found others to drive him where he needed to go so that he could remain the observer.

Once Edward and Charis were established at 168A Coast Road, Charis renamed it Wildcat Hill. Now that they had a home and needed to spend weeks there printing negatives from the first

Guggenheim Fellowship, only part of their time was taken up by photographic expeditions. Charis was writing the first draft of *California and the West*, and Edward was devoting day after day making prints in the darkroom. Of this time, Charis wrote:

> . . . we spent our days-off at Point Lobos, only a mile from our front door. Edward began by saying he was all through with it. . . . Hadn't he photographed there for six years, done every twisted cypress on the cliffs and every eroded rock on the beaches? True enough, but that had been a period of close-ups: details of rocks, fragments of trees. At first we just went out to swim and look at the scenery and walk; but Edward took his camera along in case he might see a cloud or something. He made a few negatives; we went oftener; he made more. Soon we were going out once a week and Edward was making more negatives than ever, most of them quite different from his earlier seeing of the same material. He did tide pools, landscapes, groves of cypress, seaweed and kelp in the water, breaking waves, and long views of the rugged shoreline. In the summer there was fog drifting over the rocky inlets; in the fall there were big storms to churn the foam up on the dark rocks.[44]

The fact of the matter was that, for the first time, Weston came to the peninsula as a experienced landscape photographer. Once again he saw Point Lobos with new eyes. His time away from Carmel, photographing the varied California landscape in different conditions of weather and season, prepared him for the great photographs he would take at Point Lobos in his last active decade as a photographer in a way that staying in the art colony could not.

Weston's landscapes were now more than roots and rocks he could touch and control. They were open and expansive views, such as those he had taken in Death Valley. Moving surf patterns of surging foam and tonalities of the sea in certain lighting fascinated him, as did the larger topography of Point Lobos. Even sunsets were part of his new awareness of the total coastal environment. He was working out ways to capture these new subjects from his recent landscapes for the first Guggenheim Fellowship. This was a typical Weston situation; he brought back a more sophisticated level of picture-making from every trip he made away from any of his various homes. What his earlier experience at Point Lobos had contributed

Figure 7. Edward Weston. *Wildcat Hill*, 1942 (cat. 31).

Figure 8. Edward Weston. *Point Lobos*, 1938 (cat. 1).

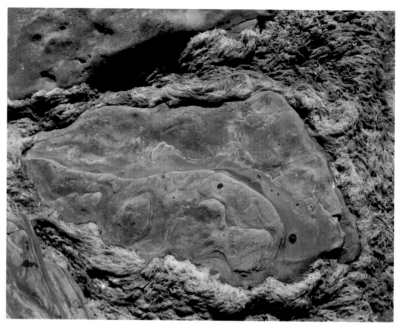

Figure 9. Edward Weston. *Untitled*, 1938 (cat. 13).

to his Guggenheim landscapes now came back to its point of origin as a highly advanced vision, and provided an opportunity he would have had at no other place.

One of the new ways of making photographs Weston brought to Point Lobos was that of seeing form not just as static, architectonic geometry or curving, organic shape: now he recognized the force of motion. He had tentatively begun this approach in cloud studies that dotted his career from his days in Mexico to his residency on Mesa Road, and to the Guggenheim Fellowships period. At Point Lobos, however, the force in motion he photographed was water.

Unlike twisted cypress or eroded rocks, which are frozen records of the effects of various forces, the ocean is in constant motion. Even distant clouds can be photographed without resorting to split-second exposures. The shorter exposures mandatory for capturing breaking and turbulent surf require bright sunlight. On December 2, 1938, Edward wrote Cole: "A beautiful high sea today. I am tempted to work on Point Lobos. My recent work there has included exposures of 1/300 second on breaking waves. Not that this is fast as others work, but it's unusual for me."[45] As light filtered through translucent water or reflected off its surface, Weston con-

fronted a different kind of picture than he had made of the opaque elements of desert landscapes. This sensibility, which also opened him to the way light affects atmosphere, was new for Weston.

Although there still appear to be graphically pronounced lines in his photographs, in reality there are only tones fronting one another, forming shapes and textures. This contrast is most obvious in the photographs he now labeled as "S" for surf in his negative numbering system. Over the next three years, he worked out the new geometry and tonality in one innovative photograph after another. These discoveries naturally affected his approach to other subjects. Rocks, whether photographed in detail or in a wider view, take on the shape of violent waves coming ashore (see fig. 8; cats. 7–8, 14) or are surrounded by seaweed mimicking calmer water streaming back out (see fig. 9).

The abundance of photographs Weston took throughout California during 1937 and 1938 can lead one to believe that subjects alone drove the adventurer-photographer to a higher refinement of his art. In *California and the West*, Charis wrote appropriately about their travel and discovery of new places; this may unintentionally reinforce the notion that subject matter was the photographer's primary concern. One must remember, however, that he was in search of "photographic subjects," not just objects or landscapes representative of California or the West such as a photojournalist might collect. For him the light that reveals form, space, and ultimately tone was paramount. Subjects like clouds or the pattern on the valley ground seen from Dante's View could further the sophistication of his vision of form and space, but if the light were not right, he would abandon the subject altogether and move on.

Weston's two years of total artistic freedom had come at the right time. He was not only ready for this good fortune, but was also in tune with his century, if we are to believe Jeffers when he identified the traits of three great Western cultures in his 1935 poem "Shine, Republic": "For the Greeks the love of beauty, for Rome of ruling; for the present age the passionate love of discovery."[46] In Weston's California landscapes from his Guggenheim period and his first landscapes after returning to Point Lobos, one perceives as never before a sense of exhilaration. Weston's world was no longer confined to a studio and its clientele. Everything had possibilities. The only limit was time and energy. He was successfully testing his theory of the mass production of original photographs. In additon his innate restlessness had been addressed in the extended voyage he had taken around the state.

Weston settled down once again and began to print the massive backlog of negatives. It was a time in which he looked for some stability. After visiting Cole at school in Seattle and meeting his fiancée, Dorothy Hermann, Edward and Charis were married on the way home, in the small town of Elk, in Mendocino County, California, on April 24, 1939. There was no prior announcement and no friends or relatives present. The couple in fact thought to keep the wedding a secret for a while, but a Carmel newspaper found out before the two returned. Charis characterized it as no big event and recalled that "Edward and I felt no need to be married, but due mainly to legal details connected with owning Wildcat Hill, it seemed the practical thing to do."[47] Nevertheless, it does signal that one of the most stable periods of Edward's life and career had begun.

At this time, Weston was also starting to figure out how to make a living from his long experience in the photographic field and what he considered his "real work." Although he would never rid himself of the portrait business, new opportunities presented themselves to lighten the load. First, Armitage suggested that the Guggenheim Foundation finance the printing of five hundred negatives of Weston's selection from the two fellowships for the Huntington Library in Pasadena, California. They agreed, and Weston began printing periodically over the next five years. Second, a series of articles on the Guggenheim Fellowship photographs and travel appeared in various publications, such as *Westways* magazine, *Magazine of Art* (Jan. 1939), *Camera Craft* (Feb. and Mar. 1939), and *U.S. Camera Annual 1940*. There were also a few interviews. With Charis as ghost writer for these articles, a continuing stream of essays on portraiture, trees, lighting, and not being a purist appeared in the same two years, as well as the Westons' complete rewriting of F. J. Mortimer's article "Photographic Art" in 1940 for *Encyclopedia Britannica*.[48]

At the end of 1940, the book they had worked on for so long, *California and the West*, appeared to favorable reviews and paid the couple royalties. This was satisfying, as Charis remembered: "We soon heard that California and the West was the first really successful book of photographic reproductions. It was decidedly different from others we had seen, not being an art book. Not only did it have plenty of story, but it was reasonably priced at $3.75. There was a second printing within two years, when the price was raised to $5.00. Edward finally got his wish to cut back on portrait sittings. Now he could be pickier about who sat for his camera."[49] The reproductions were satisfactory, given it was not meant as an art book, and Charis was pleased, as it proved to her the importance of her role beyond being a wife and note-taking assistant. In addition to income from publishing, Weston taught a workshop in Yosemite with Ansel Adams in June 1940 and another in the fall of the same year. He began to take individual students and continued to promote sales of his photographs through exhibitions.

Weston had now entered a new period of his life and career. Although his photographs were still about discovery and freedom, they would soon begin to touch on deeper personal issues, subtly revealing his state of mind. He refused to say that his work reflected his own emotional peace or turmoil, still believing that photography was primarily an objective record of what is possible to see. Nevertheless, his photographs had changed, as had he.

Imogen Cunningham. *Edward Weston at Point Lobos*, 1945.

Weston's early days in Carmel, the time of the Guggenheim Fellowships, and the first years in the Carmel Highlands form a classic middle period of a talented and prolific artist. An outline sketch of a career for artists who maintain their vigorous creative drive into old age might read something like this: In the first period, artists begin to discover their talent, the world, and themselves. They test new techniques and seek first experiences, applying little caution to their encounters. It is an exhilarating period of experiment and appetite. In the middle, or second period, artists develop skill and then virtuosity in their chosen medium. This itself becomes a major factor in stimulating their imagination. When all goes well, it is as if virtuosity and imagination are in step; an advance in one is followed by an advance in the other. It is a satisfying period of focus and distinction. The imagination finds new approaches and virtuosity turns those ideas into pictures. Then, the order of this process can reverse, as virtuosity finds a new approach

IV. THE THIRD PERIOD

and the imagination must resolve it into a picture. These sequential events, in whichever order, help to explain why Weston often said that what he was doing intuitively as a photographer was always ahead of what he could write about it.[50]

Weston's second period ran from the age of thirty-eight, when he moved to Mexico, to 1944, when, at the age of fifty-eight, he began producing a different kind of photograph of Point Lobos. In the case of most artists, the second period is characterized by an enhanced confidence, as youthful obstinacy becomes artful certainty. For Weston this time was one in which new treatments of new subjects, such as cypress roots or vegetables, were seen by him as welcome challenges. And it is in this period that he permanently shifted his goals: rather than concerning himself with the *interpretation* of the subject, he focused on its *presentation*. Typical of this second period is the expansion of content of the works beyond technical accomplishment and superficial meaning; they now represent a point of departure for intellectual responses by various individuals. If Weston tried to capture the "significant form" or "universal rhythms" of common objects, his friends still made their own interpretations of his objective representations. It was fine when they compared inanimate roots to flames, but when they linked the shapes of peppers to sexual

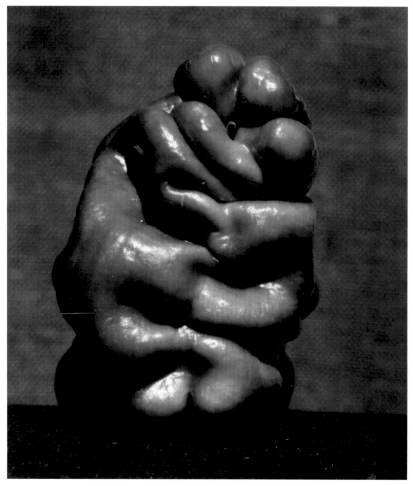

Figure 10. Edward Weston. *Pepper*, 1929.

Figure 11. Edward Weston. *Nude*, 1935.

desires (see fig. 10), the photographer felt he had to object. He did not want his photographs to symbolize a state of mind, as Alfred Stieglitz claimed for the series of cloud studies he called *Equivalents*. Nevertheless, beyond the likeness of the pepper's sensual curves to the human body (see fig. 11), this reading was hard to resist for friends who knew of Weston's many love affairs.

Artists of the second period are often characterized as having the virtue of extended youthfulness with a touch of adolescence. Western culture has historically equated the creative impulse with youthful habits of playful thought and experiment, and since the Romantic period has glorified artists who challenge tradition. There are abundant expressions of this attitude. In one of his famous essays, published in the early seventeenth century, Francis Bacon, describing youth, wrote, "Imaginations stream in their minds better, and, as it were, more divinely. . . . Young men are fitter to invent, than to judge; fitter for execution, than for counsel, and fitter for new projects, than for settled business."[51]

Typical of the beginning and middle of the second period of a creative career is the destruction of earlier work that the artist deems immature. This is less true in scientific fields than in the arts, where the value of a work over time may be determined by the maturity of the artist's life experience when it was made.[52] Weston scraped the emulsion from his pictorialist negatives in his mid-thirties and used the glass plates as window panes. In 1925, when he was nearly forty, he destroyed his earliest daybooks, an act he later regretted when he wanted to look back on the man he once was.[53] At the end of the second period, artists often experience a feeling of being buoyed and carried on by success or prowess. Audiences, publishers, and dealers do not want successful and popular artists to abandon their known styles and identities. Neither do artists want to abandon what they have learned to do so well. Thus, many look horizontally for new subjects, even new techniques, to conquer in their established style rather than developing a wholly new attitude that would add a depth of meaning to what they have at their command.[54]

The model of the individual ever young, inventive, and iconoclastic, however, ill prepares artists for making substantial contributions in the third period of creativity, old age. It also ill prepares those who view art for what a great artist may become late in life. Weston himself bragged about his youthfulness in his daybooks and quoted from them in his later publications. Likewise, historians and scholars have used the text of the daybooks to explain his whole career. This has often contributed to the misreading of the character and importance of his work in Weston's last active years as a photographer.

Because of the stereotypical characterizations of old age as a time of diminished powers and health, confronting its arrival is often an act of elaborate postponement. As Betty Friedan astutely described from study and experience, "The problem is, first of all, how to break through the cocoon of our illusory youth and risk a new stage in life, where there are no prescribed role models to follow, no guideposts, no rigid rules or visible rewards, to step out into the true existential unknown of these new years of life now open to us, and to find our own terms for living it."[55] In this last phase, a self-reflective capacity becomes a creative act itself. Virginia Woolf anticipated this third period when she observed in *Mrs. Dalloway*: "The compensation of growing . . . was simply this: that the passions remain as strong as ever, but one had gained—at last!—the power which adds the supreme flavour to existence,—the power of taking hold of experience, of turning it round, slowly, in the light."[56]

The third period is different from the first two, not in degree of creative activity but in kind. Unlike the imagination, virtuosity—the way a new idea finds its ultimate physical form—has a limit. When the imagination advances further than virtuosity can follow, many creative individuals are trapped in old ways of applying their skills to new ideas. It is a situation without a name. Artists entering the third period sooner or later recognize that they have never before encountered anything like it. Those of modest ambition or waning talent are not profoundly bothered by the problems it presents, as they and their undemanding audiences are satisfied with comfortable variations on established themes. But as our culture prepares us so inadequately for the shift, even perceptive and gifted artists may wonder if this is yet another crisis to be solved with yet another extension of virtuosity.

It is rare that artists can anticipate what is different about the third period. They generally reflect on it only after they are well into it, finding an examination of their own life experience as the primary advantage in creating new work. It is a time in which judgment acquired from maturity overshadows the youthful traits of wild freedom, new discovery, audacious invention, and the prideful display of skill. The third period still requires virtuosity and imagination, but demands that the imagination interact with personal experience. In the fields of teaching, ruling, and healing, the word characterizing knowledge, experience, and imagination is *wisdom*. The field of art has no analogous term for what is an amalgam of talent, experience, and imagination.

The poet Wallace Stevens recognized the third period and gave primacy to the imagination when he wrote:

Over all these the mighty imagination triumphs
Like a trumpet and says, in this season of memory,
When the leaves fall like things mournful of the past,

Keep quiet in the heart, O wild bitch. O mind
Gone wild, be what he tells you to be: Puella.
Write pax *across the window pane. And then*

Be still. The summarium in excelsis *begins . . .*
Flame, sound fury composed . . . Hear what he says,
The dauntless master, as he starts the human tale.[57]

Stevens dealt with the onset of the third period by recognizing a higher authority, a divinity to which he felt only the imagination can lead us. For Weston, who remained an atheist, the work of the imagination was its own end and satisfaction. Stevens urged us to listen and be receptive to the voices not of conquerors but of peacemakers. Weston and Stevens would seem to have agreed on this point, as the photographer after 1944 appears to have been at ease with the idea that photographs were all around him rather than at great distances achieved after strenuous travel. Stevens recognized the third period as one of memory, which may be more characteristic of a poet's realm than that of certain photographers. Poets may also come earlier to the level of self-consciousness required to be creative in old age than photographers, especially those like Weston, who work exclusively with objects of tangible and immediate reality.

Whether one is a poet or a photographer, an expanded self-consciousness of one's existence eventually does come with age. Great artists do not deny that they are now fitter to judge than to invent, and they exercise their new powers in their work. When poets or photographers in this third period apply their judgment to their experience of the last twenty years, they view an accomplished self who is entering mid-life. When those in the middle period look back, they have only a green and youthful beginning to draw upon, thus their greater reliance on invention than on judgment.

The personal experience of individuals, so suspect in the sciences, is both the undeniable authority in the arts in Western cultures and its glory. Far Eastern cultures in contrast give more respect to longer apprenticeships and the traditions of the past formed by a consensus of experience. In the Asian view, the most revolutionary changes are expected not at the beginning or middle of a career but rather toward its end. This opinion of artists' development is evident in a 1588 description of the ideal training of a Japanese tea master, thought to be drawn from the life of Sen-no-Rikyu:

> From the age of 15 to 30 leave everything up to the master. From the age of 30 to 40 distinguish one's own taste following one's inclinations in preparation, instruction, and conversation letting half of all one does be original. From 40 to 50 become as different from one's master as East from West, creating a personal style and gaining a name for skill, for this is the means of revitalizing the way of tea. From 50 to 60 transform tea altogether as one's master did before one, like pouring water out of one vessel into another, and making one's performance as a master the standard in every respect.[58]

Weston was fifty-one in 1937, when he received his first Guggenheim Fellowship. By the tea master's chronology, he should have been poised to transform photography altogether. If he recognized the situation or even thought about it at all, he would have considered himself ready. Changing photography altogether is a tall order at any time, and in truth not every great tea master completely transformed *chado*—the Way of Tea—either. There is, nevertheless, something to say for Weston in this regard.

Before Weston's career in Carmel, one is hard pressed to find a true practitioner of the photographic medium, not just a wealthy amateur, who reduced his or her life to the bare necessities in order to maximize opportunity and condition the mind to concentrate on little else than the making of original photographs. In this Weston resembles a tea master. Like Japan's *chajin*—those who devote their lives to following the Way of Tea—the photographer became almost monklike in his fixation on subsuming his lifestyle to his goal. Jeffers singled out this trait in an appreciation of Weston he wrote in 1947: "He knows exactly what he wants to do, and he does it as simply as possible. He is not interested in the affectations and showmanship that distract many talented persons; I think he has never even been interested in having a career, but only in doing his work well."[59]

Other friends whose lives and careers imposed demands beyond their practice as artists, such as photographer Ansel Adams or curators Beaumont and Nancy Newhall, admired and even envied the Spartan life that Weston had created and guarded for himself. They initially responded by wishing they wanted to change their own lives, as Weston had, but found themselves committed to an existence that required constant interaction with the practical, commercial world. They also had to deal with the history, management, and intrepretation of art for others.[60] Weston's example of directing his full attention to his art by simplifying his lifestyle and not wasting time on peripheral matters not only inspired friends and visitors, but has continued to serve as the primary model to key figures in photography wanting to devote themselves entirely to their art. That much of the field he changed completely.

The tea master's chronology ends at the age of sixty, around the time that the third period begins for modern artists. Although Sen-no-Rikyu lived to be seventy,[61] the medieval Japanese may have had difficulty assigning a virtue and duty to a master in his sixties.

When passing sixty, after all, tea masters like artists enter the period *following* the one that has usually had the most impact historically. Even if great artists transform an aspect of how their field will be considered by all who come after them, they do not necessarily cease working. As many great artists proceed into old age, they give back to the field and others only part of what they do, reserving a part solely for themselves. This seems to have been the case with Sen-no-Rikyu, who through his sixties followed an even humbler form of *chado* than he had before. Artists who once spoke so eagerly as masters to the wide world often turn inward not in selfish disregard, but rather to examine what the creative life means not to their admirers but to themselves. The aging Michelangelo, in his last *Pietà*, and the deaf Beethoven, in his final quartets, are the examples most often cited in Western culture.[62] In such cases, we are more eavesdroppers than intended audience. The latter part of a late career can be a private realm and the work hard to appreciate for those who expect that art's purpose must always be the communication of one sensibility to another. Of course not all artists who recognize that the third period is upon them invert their concentration so completely or seek what seems a hermit's truth. The examples of Milton, Verdi, Monet, and Yeats readily come to mind. Nevertheless, the unique core of the third period for great artists is the new freedom they attain either to actively address an audience or to confront the last vestiges of the imagination alone, appearing to do little that speaks to others; "inanimate in an inert savoir" is the phrase Stevens created for this state of mind.[63]

Weston did not work far into the third period. The disease that Cole observed in his father's labored movements would worsen and prevent that. There are, nonetheless, indications in his last photographs that the culminating period had begun.

Clarence John Laughlin. *Incantation against Love's End. A Portrait of Edward Weston*, 1941.

As early as 1940, some of Weston's photographs began to look different. The photograph *Sea, Point Lobos* (cat. 21), which he took looking out to a calm, leaden sea choked with the floating kelp that previous storms had uprooted, is indicative of a new way of approaching his subjects. Here, the normally controling photographer seems passive: the composition is less aggressively constructed, as Weston concentrated primarily on creating yet another tone for the coastal waters. This time tone, more than composition, would convey his feelings. The open vista of the image, with its distant horizon, is peaceful, but the water's particular gray color is what gives the picture a sense of foreboding. Another disjunctive contradiction can be seen in *China Cove, Point Lobos* (cat. 20), taken the same year. This composition is not open but confined. Its focus is split between two distinct objects: an irregular, black rock and a swirling pattern of kelp brightened by reflected sunlight. Although the scintillating light on waves whipped by the wind has

V. THE WAR YEARS

an invigorating quality to it, there is within the boundary of the frame a sense of mystery for all the abundance and contradiction it contains. Here, Weston gave light a brighter, more spiritual quality than when he photographed the sorrowful gray of slow water. One cannot help but sense that these scenes draw their power from his own, inner landscapes. One can now more easily see him, in this single masterpiece, as treating nature's awe as the dark, hard, ragged-edged outline of masculine temper or its sublimity as the sinuous, emollient filaments of feminine caress.

The perceived moods and the place Weston made for contrasting objects and emotions in his photographs and psyche were beginning to be noticed by his associates at the time. A trained eye could sense this change as Weston established a new balance of elements during his rediscovery of Point Lobos. Beaumont and Nancy Newhall paid a visit to the region for the first time in the summer of 1940, with Ansel Adams. Nancy recorded the experience in her notes:

> We went to Point Lobos with Edward, and to see Lobos with Edward was to see Dante's *Inferno* and *Paradiso* simultaneously. The vast ocean, dangerous and serene, pale emerald and clear

sapphire, sucking in and out of caves full of anemones; tidepools flickering with life or drying inward into crystals and filaments of salt; the cliffs starred with stonecrop; the living cypress dark as thunder clouds, with silver skeletons of the ancient dead gleaming among them . . . .[64]

Whether or not Weston was entering a new period based on the trajectory of his own career or on his inner self, outside events would soon determine the course of his life and what photographs he would take. The most obvious event was the bombing of Pearl Harbor on December 7, 1941, which marked the beginning of a new period for nearly all Americans, whether they were prepared for it or not. Jeffers saw it coming. His premonitions in the period before the war were not subtle. As early as 1935, Jeffers had developed a Cassandra-like voice in his poetry that would cause his popularity to decline. Some of his lines became nightmares of fatalistic verse:

> I would burn my right hand in a slow fire
> To change the future . . . I should do foolishly. The beauty of modern
> Man is not in the persons but in the
> Disastrous rhythm, the heavy and mobile masses, the dance of the
> Dream-led masses down the dark mountain.[65]

If the poet was ahead of the photographer in voicing a darkened mood, it was not for long, according to Weston's biographer, Ben Maddow. When the United States entered World War II, Edward and Charis Weston were in Wilmington, Delaware, working their way down the East Coast, in the seventh month of a major commission. Early in 1941, Armitage had helped to arrange for Weston to illustrate a deluxe reprinting of Walt Whitman's *Leaves of Grass* for the Limited Editions Book Club.[66] The fee was barely sufficient for travel and material expenses it took to get the Westons around the country between May 1941 and January 1942. Nevertheless, it was a welcome opportunity, for it was almost like a third Guggenheim Fellowship, in that it allowed Edward and Charis to travel together again with some freedom in the choice of subjects and approach. Once more Weston was living the life of an "adventurer on a voyage

of discovery ready to receive fresh impressions, eager for fresh horizons."[67] Invigorating as the Whitman commission was supposed to be, Maddow characterized some of the Whitman photographs as "quite frankly, funereal."[68] The historian and critic Alan Trachtenberg recently wrote of these commissioned photographs: "Predominantly, however, the feeling is elegiac. . . . The sense of age and aging hangs over the pictures made in 1941–42. . . . Old places, old things, old faces settle into an impression of inertness. . . . Landscapes heavy with clouds seem brooding."[69] Writing in the 1970s and 1990s, respectively, Maddow and Trachtenberg of course knew how Weston's career would end, and they detected signs of its coming. Certainly, nothing of this sort was expressed the year the photographs were published.[70] The book did not communicate a darkened mood to most viewers, for the reproductions, which were not under Weston's control, were printed a bit lighter than his originals.[71] The description of change in these photographs might also have been caused by misreading the over-inked reprint of 1976, or darker prints made toward the end of the artist's life. If there was a shift, it is certainly slight compared to the deepening anguish of Jeffers's contemporary poems.[72]

Trachtenberg did, however, qualify his analysis by saying that what appeared changed in Weston's photographs were "nuances, subtleties of tone, slight shifts of compositional emphasis."[73] Perhaps Weston was worried. Having heard rumors of Japanese submarines twenty miles off the California coast and the shelling of an oil installation at Santa Barbara, he wondered if he might find the Carmel Highlands evacuated on his return. Charis was eager to continue the trip but deferred to Edward, who was also anxious about his draft-eligible sons.[74]

If Weston's photographs of 1941 are funereal or elegiac, it may be because of Weston's changing state of mind. Personally, Edward and Charis started to have serious marital problems during the trip that affected their partnership. As Charis related:

> The success of *California and the West* had given me a keen appetite for more opportunities to exercise my talent. I was a full partner, or so I thought, and my role in the partnership required a kind of exploration that couldn't be done given our pace. . . . He didn't want to waste time on a side trip that might give him nothing. A tightness

in his voice warned me that, as far as he was concerned, the discussion was closed. In the heat of the moment, he wanted to put me back in my place as his younger follower and assistant.[75]

Later in the trip, Charis became infatuated with one of their hosts in New England, a literary man who, as she remembered, had "no limits to his horizons, in thinking, reading, or feeling, and I basked in his obvious admiration of me as a person and an author."[76] This situation was something that Weston might have recognized as typical of his own behavior in his younger years. Although she stated clearly in her memoirs that she was not unfaithful, Charis came to believe that Edward might have worried that she would "abandon ship—stranding him a continent away from home, with a car full of equipment and a project to finish."[77]

The changes in the photographs may also have been prompted by the fact that the commission required Weston to work in twenty-three states other than California, in different cultures, on different coasts, and in different weather. Photographically, Weston was frustrated by the onset of winter in New England. In the dull, cloudy atmosphere, celebrated landscapes, such as those along the coast of Maine, did not compare well to Point Lobos. Weston was used to winters where clouds delivered rain that made the hills green, or to a shift of wind direction that brought dramatic waves crashing upon outcrops of stone in a season clear of fog.[78]

Professionally, the Whitman trip was a specific commission, not the free and open exploration that the Guggenheim Fellowships had allowed. Weston had to contend with history, other photographic studies of the United States, and Whitman's powerful idea of America as he tried to form his own.[79] All through his journey, Weston had to rely on others far more than before. In almost every region, he was beholden to locals to learn what he could of the region during his brief stays. Most outspoken and opinionated of his guides was the New Orleans photographer Clarence John Laughlin, who had his own agenda for what he thought should be photographed and how. Weston photographed the ruins of the Woodlawn and Belle Grove plantations with Laughlin on August 10, 1941, but the visiting Californian was relieved to return to Belle Grove the next day under the guidance of his friends Don and Bea Prendergast, getting away both from Laughlin and the tourist-infested French Quarter.

Even if Laughlin, who had a proclivity for the subject of death and otherworldly things (see fig. 12), took Weston to his favorite decayed antebellum plantations, Weston did not see such subjects as either morbid or spooky (see fig. 13).[80] Neither did Weston believe that his photographs of dead animals indicated a preoccupation with the subject, or even his numerous other dead subjects: bleached-white skulls in the desert, a human corpse, trees uprooted by violent storms, burnt stumps, dilapidated buildings in ghost towns, debris of all kinds, driftwood on eroded rocks, discarded abalone shells, wrecked automobile bodies on the beach, broken wagon wheels in weeds, a fox on a wooden plank, and knots of dried kelp. There was another explanation.

Weston argued against what seemed obvious to others, as he had argued against the sexual interpretations of his peppers. He insisted that dead subjects were just part of his larger observation of life. As late as 1946, he defended this position to Minor White, who had written of death as a motif in Weston's later work: "As for Death as a theme—it certainly didn't start with the dead man in the Colorado Desert. Before 1910 I did skulls and dead Joshua trees on the Mojave Desert. But then as now, Death was not a theme—it was just part of life—as simple as that."[81] Yet another point of view comes from the novelist Mary Austin when she described the attraction that the desert holds for men: "There is something incomprehensible to the man-mind in the concurrence of death and beauty . . . . Mind you, it is mostly men who go into the desert, who love it past all reasonableness, slack their ambitions, cast off old usages, neglect their families because of the pulse and beat of a life laid bare to its thews and sinews."[82]

"Life laid bare" and holding still for the view camera were situations too perfect for Weston as a photographer to pass up, whether he was in the prime of his life or near its end. But in order to learn something significant about his attitude toward life, death, and art as he entered old age, one must give up such facile symbols. What is more important to identify is the way Weston made photographs in response to both his internal mental condition and the inescapable situation he faced from the outside world.

The bombing of Pearl Harbor left the West Coast unprotected. The wartime mentality and threat of air attack were factors that now started to shape Weston's thoughts and activities. After several

Figure 12. Clarence John Laughlin. *Time Phantasm*, 1941.

Figure 13. Edward Weston. *Woodlawn, Louisiana*, 1941.

months of printing a backlog of the Whitman commission negatives (Brett had developed them as his father sent them back to California), Edward followed Charis's lead and joined the Ground Observer Corps, U.S. Army Air Forces, IV Fighter Command, Aircraft Warning Service. His months-long periods of travel for making new photographs ended. At the time, he could not know that they would never reoccur.

The few photographs that Weston took at Point Lobos in 1942, before it was declared off-limits for civilians, were close-up studies: dead birds (see fig. 20) and eroded sandstone rocks with disorienting, figurelike shapes (cat. 28) and splatters of tar (cat. 29). Even the most abstract of his photographs at the time, *Salt-encrusted Rock, Point Lobos* (fig. 14), bears an uncanny, although unintended,

resemblance to aerial bombardment photographs (see fig. 15), as scale is purposely ambiguous. While the subjects of these photographs may again seem facile symbols of death, they were now either directly or indirectly part of nearly every photograph Weston took. The insistent subject may be indicative of the new mix of his emotions, as his imagination was no longer distracted or fired by new discoveries of places he had never seen. Even in his retreat on Wildcat Hill, the presence of the war was inescapable. As Charis remembered, "The war was very much with us, as it was with everyone we knew, and affected us some way or other around the clock."[83] On May 24, 1943, Edward wrote a letter in which he described his state of mind. Addressing it to Cole, he sent it to all four of his sons:

Figure 14. Edward Weston. *Salt-encrusted Rock, Point Lobos*, 1942 (cat. 30).

Figure 15. American Expeditionary Forces Under the Command of Edward Steichen. *Mine Craters, Combres Hill*, 1915/18.

The question you posit in re the artist and his activities in war time has already been answered by you; you had to return to your creative expression. And in like manner Neil went on with his, so did Brett, so did I. . . . Despite war, even because of it, the biological urge goes on, and so does the creative urge—perhaps in keenly intensified form. Whether or not your work can't help being influenced indirectly; so pay no attention to those who say "Ivory tower" just answer "Ivory Soap to you." If you wish to do propaganda for or against "-ism" fine; but don't imagine that the propaganda isn't there, however it may be hidden. If the law enforcing agents could only understand the significance of some music they would ban it, burn it. Communism might be seen in Bach or Fascism in Wagner.[84]

With Point Lobos closed and gas rationing in effect, Weston's world was restricted as never before. Normally, a period after a long photographic trek would have produced an explosive activity at Point Lobos. Instead, Weston began orchestrating tableaux, "backyard set-ups," as Nancy Newhall called them.[85] Friends claimed the result of this stage management to be surrealistic, a characterization he rightly denied.[86] Although they were often spontaneous reactions

to objects and situations, which was not a change in his way of reacting to the world for him, the tableaux were a new kind of photograph. To them he gave a new kind of title, not his typical identification of place and date. He did not have time or opportunity to stage more than half a dozen. His favorites were *Civilian Defense* (cat. 26),[87] which is sometimes called *Victory* and shows Charis nude on a couch wearing a gas mask; *My Little Gray Home in the West* (cat. 37),[88] in which Charis is standing nude, nonchalantly holding Edward's Carmel studio sign as a fig leaf, with her brother Leon blithely playing a recorder from an open window; *Exposition of Dynamic Symmetry* (cat. 38),[89] which features four friends holding arbitrary objects from the windows of the facade of a two-story wooden house; and *Good Neighbor Policy* (cat. 36),[90] which depicts a figurine with arms outstretched as if blessing a six-pack of Dr. Pepper soda. As Charis recollected, Edward "did not seek out messages"; perhaps, he was being satirically playful, making light of photographs that delivered messages overtly, especially propaganda images, which were now plentiful.[91]

If these photographs were reactions to Weston's frustrations, they also tested his freedom of expression. He did not want to feel locked into a predictable system of photography, producing what

Figure 16. Edward Weston. *William Edmundson*, 1941.

Figure 17. Edward Weston. *Neil*, 1942 (cat. 33).

his viewers believed a Weston photograph should be. He had anar-
chistic tendencies that, in his mind, were not strictly political but
a natural part of what he thought crucial to the make up of an
artist.[92] In these whimsical and ironic "set-ups," Weston was not
concerned with "freshly conquered fields," but with his own existence. Not everything was affected by his new defiance, however.
He made a clear distinction between what was photographed in an
artificial or domestic setting and what was essentially wild in nature
and thus to be revered.

Although the tableaux represent the most conspicuous stylistic
change of this period, Weston was also making an entirely different kind of image: portraits of his immediate family (see fig. 17).
Unlike the tableaux, these photographs carry Weston's more profound, personal feelings of caring and concern. He did not take these
family portraits to be overtly clever or satirical like the tableaux. If
anything they resemble several of the respectful portraits he had
made during the Whitman commission of people posed in their own
surroundings (see fig. 16). Again, Weston brought something back
to Wildcat Hill from his travels elsewhere. Although the portraits
of his sons are less formally rigid, he used this new motif of portrait

and environment to pose them in activities in which they were already
occupied: fixing roofs, whittling, or chopping wood. Although Weston
composed photographs of his sons in various situations, he seemed
to be both revealing and completing something within himself in
these new portraits. They speak of his own pride in masculine
prowess, now complemented with a sense of loving regard. Later,
he typically understated the meaning of these images: "Of course
the war did terrific things to all of us, with four boys in it I couldn't
deny this—but my new figures in landscapes—or portraits they
really are—were not the result of the order of my life breaking
down. Rather I was sick to death of doing portraits under a 45
degree light, which I had done professionally for almost forty years,
and because I was barred from Point Lobos."[93]

The photographs of Weston's sons did not become exaggerated,
sentimental portraits made in a time of emotional tension. In them
he used all his objective photographic skills and perception; that
they are also deeply affectionate does not detract from their being
some of the most accomplished portraits of his career. Weston now
saw his sons not only living life on their own, but contributing to
a joy and emotional satisfaction he treasured and needed more and

more. Not surprisingly, given the mounting tensions in his marriage, his nudes of Charis (cats. 54–58, 62), although still highly innovative, appear increasingly less passionate and direct, revealing the state of his mind, and perhaps hers.[94]

Weston, who once championed showing "the thing itself" in photographs, considered his state of mind to be a private matter and not the prime content of his work. Nevertheless, as he aged, it became a factor of increasing importance in his approach to his photography. In one of his last statements about his art, he wrote: "When I was very young—say in my early forties—I defined art as 'outer expression of inner growth.' . . . I can't define art any better, today, but my work has changed."[95]

These changes were noticeable both in Weston's choice of subjects and in his treatment of them. The tableaux represented a search for another direction and were suited to his straight, unmanipulated technique, which could easily couple objective records with intellectual ideas. His family portraits, rendered by the same technique, are more emotional and subjective, however. As these changes took place, the photographer may have wondered whether his unrivaled virtuosity in the medium was suitable for expressing the more complicated inner self as it struggled with the emotions prompted by war, a failing marriage, and increasing health problems. If anything, the objectivity for which he was famous would have seemed to his contemporary critics the perfect tool for masking such emotions.

Weston's highly sophisticated photographic formalism, based first on line and then on space, and increasingly rendered through photographic tones, was a magnificent achievement equaled only by a few other talents in the field, such as Ansel Adams and Paul Strand. Edward's portraits of his sons demonstrate that, as the photographer entered old age, his genius enabled him to transcend the gap of meaning between two conditions: one of seeing the world as an external reality of inexhaustible beauty and power that he felt needed discovery and conquest; and the other of exploring and nurturing his own psyche, with its wealth of emotional experience and conflict. Formerly, Weston's daybooks had served the purpose of holding and releasing his pent-up feelings. Some of that inner dialogue now began to appear in his photographs. He would judge his ideas and photographs strictly on personal terms and not by what anyone else in the field thought. It was a condition that was both liberating and demanding: success on his own terms could mean even more, as could failure.

Ansel Adams. *Edward Weston*, 1945.

On January 1, 1944, Weston wrote Nancy Newhall: "You guess that the war has upset me. I don't think so, not more than the average dislocation. . . . As to Pt. Lobos, it has been open to the public for months, but I have had no desire to work there." [96] Perhaps, he was still depressed from being confined for so long to his "palatial shack" as his marriage fell apart. But if Weston thought he was done with Point Lobos because of emotional difficulties at home, he was wrong.

Considering the limitations imposed on his freedom, 1944 turned out to be productive for Weston. From the pattern of his career—continued inspiration after a photographic journey—it was the year one might have expected to happen after his return to Carmel from the Whitman commission in 1942. His desire not to work at Point Lobos did not last long, as his mind's eye began to imagine photographs that could both contain a universal form and reflect his state of mind.

VI. THE LAST YEARS

In addition to Weston's renewed activity at Point Lobos, another photographic pursuit came to occupy his time. Finding they were happier when working together on a project, Edward and Charis collaborated on a second book, which was about the tribe of semiwild cats they kept in and around the house. The substantial text of *The Cats of Wildcat Hill* is accompanied by twenty tour-de-force photographs that Edward took with his eight-by-ten-inch view camera in 1944 and 1945 (see fig. 7 and cat. 39). [97] The photography was a monumental technical challenge, as it was difficult to get the cats to hold still for the necessary exposures and to capture their expressive features. But Weston had developed great patience as a portrait photographer and had already gained experience in a directorial approach from the tableaux photographs.

In 1944 Chandler, Brett, and Cole began their military service and Neil joined the Merchant Marines. For the next year or so, the opportunity to see and photograph his sons—who, with Point Lobos, had become his most meaningful subjects—was reduced to the measure of a few holidays. Their tours of duty also deprived Weston of his sons' emotional support. His life with Charis on Wildcat Hill was not improving. As she recounted: "There were no scenes—no battles, vituperation, accusations, tears, or periods

Figure 18. Edward Weston. *Red Rock Canyon*, 1937.

Figure 19. Edward Weston. *Granite Cliff, Point Lobos*, 1944 (cat. 45).

of short-lived truce. Rather, a portcullis had dropped between us and I could find no way through. . . . Fleeing from silence, I filled my days with as many outside activities as possible. . . . Although we still slept together, we seldom made love, partly because the act of joining without fully communing was too painful a reminder of how far our relationship had deteriorated."[98]

Later in the year, Weston received an honor and an opportunity to organize the past and present masterpieces of his long career into a retrospective exhibition. It proved to be less than the exhilaration that one might have imagined it should have been. Weston's emotional distractions at home had begun to show. Nancy Newhall was now completing the retrospective at the Museum of Modern Art, New York, that her husband had begun before his military tour of duty. It should have been a joyous occasion all around, as the Westons had become close friends with the Newhalls. Although working on projects with Charis helped their relationship, the retrospective was not turning out to be an important goal for Edward artistically. Writing to Nancy about one of the museum's supporting patrons whom he admired, Edward tried to excuse his lack of enthusiasm: "Yes, Dave McAlpin is a 'swell guy.' You know that I am really going through with this

show for such as he, and you, and Beau, and a few more: otherwise I would much rather make new photographs, play with cats, work on place, aid the war effort, or just lie in the sun—don't misunderstand; I appreciate the opportunity and the honor, but the older I get, the less I seek out publicity."[99] Even if his unhappy marriage affected his spirit, he was, as he said, less eager to focus his energies on anything other than his own personal pursuits, a trait common to creative individuals in old age as they recognize the value of the time left to them and their independence.

Given all that was happening in his family life, it is not surprising that Weston's new photographs of Point Lobos have a darker, more pensive mood. What had once been nuanced now darkened into cold stone (see fig. 19). Weston started with an idea from *Red Rock Canyon* (fig. 18), made during the first year of the Guggenheim trip, in which he allowed a plane of stone texture to spread across the ground glass in a rather featureless way. He had left that idea undeveloped. Now he let the whole cliffside settle in his view camera (see cats. 41–48), perhaps expecting its myriad components to compose themselves and recover for him an ancient story of granite disfigured by outside forces.

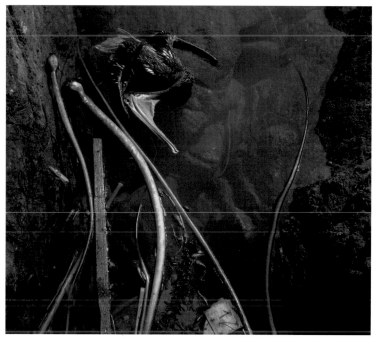

Figure 20. Edward Weston. *Dead Pelican, Point Lobos*, 1942 (cat. 27).

Figure 21. Edward Weston. *Dead Pelican, Point Lobos*, 1945 (cat. 60).

Jeffers too had studied rocks and identified with them:

> . . . *I have much in common*
> *with these old rockheads,*
> *Old comrades, I too have escaped and stand.*
> *I have shared in my time the human illusions,*
>   *the muddy foolishness*
> *And craving passions, but something thirty years ago*
>   *pulled me*
> *Out of the tide-wash; I must not even pretend*
> *To be one of the people. I must stand here*
> *Alone with open eyes in the clearing air growing old. . . .*[100]

Weston's tack was a bit different. The photographer now avoided the singular outcrop as a symbol and looked to the mass of the cliff. The battered cliff, to be sure, is an obvious metaphor for Weston's life in 1944 and 1945, even for the country's, but again that interpretation is too facile. If we examine the photographer's *approach* rather than his *subject*, we can detect something more. In these works, there is no sense of personal rage, as in Jeffers's poems of the period, or of the heightened emotion that Abstract Expressionist painters would later introduce in similar flat-field compositions of spreading and assaulted shapes. Rather, there is a certain feeling of resignation. Not the resignation of defeat, but the kind Stevens described as writing "pax across the window pane." Perhaps, in the case of the photographer, a more accurate word is acceptance. In these pictures, Weston was speaking more to himself than to us. It is as if he were finally ready to listen in silent reverence to what stood before him and not call upon his considerable virtuosity to command it into a photographic composition of line or space. Tone now dominated his photographs of Point Lobos, resulting in their having more of a pronounced mood than they had in the past. Having solved nothing for himself in the highly directed tableau photographs or in the portraits of cats, this was his step forward into his late period, his way out of an end that he had not foreseen. Had he been much younger, Weston would have taken scores of photographs in this new way. Now a few images of deeper meaning were enough.

Figure 22. Edward Weston. *Nude*, 1945 (cat. 54).

Figure 23. Edward Weston. *Prologue to a Sad Spring*, 1920.

In 1945 Weston photographed a dead pelican floating in a tide pool of discarded sticks, kelp, and dark transparent water (fig. 21).[101] The symbol of death in this photograph continued from others before, graced as they often are with fluid shapes associated with growth and the movement of life. But here Weston stood back further from the bird than he had with similar subjects in the past. Looking down he framed the whole scene around the pelican in a flat composition without perspective. There before him was the result of another struggle of a life against superior power. The 1945 pelican photograph is about death of course, but is not a metaphor for the photographer's. More than ever, Weston still saw his subject as part of the larger cycle of life. The internal patterns of a dead pelican and its feathers taken three years earlier (fig. 20) gave way to one that began to address not universal geometries of nature but its sublimity.

Edward stood back emotionally as well in framing his nudes of Charis (see cat. 54–58, 62). His eye was still inventive but now dispassionate, empty of desire, and devoid of recrimination. The inner complications he brought to these few photographs, far from weakening his imagination, asked it to do even more, to expect impossibilities, such as making nudes of a woman whose love he was losing and whom he seldom touched. No longer trapped by the flare of passion that needed the discipline of technique to check it, he played no clever compositional games of linear geometry as he had in his first nudes of Charis in 1934. Nor did he deny the psychological situation outside of the frame and let it impinge on the body within it as a mood. In making his last nudes of Charis, Edward seemed to be in a more self-reflective stage and may have wondered, as W. B. Yeats had near the same age:

Does the imagination dwell the most
Upon a woman won or a woman lost?
If on the lost, admit you turned aside
From a great labyrinth out of pride,
Cowardice, some silly over-subtle thought
Or anything called conscience once;
And that if memory recur, the sun's
Under eclipse and the day blotted out.[102]

In one photograph (cat. 55), Weston posed Charis as a distant figurine fetchingly lit behind the lattice of a window as if in a museum vitrine. In another (fig. 22), he faced her frontally, once again opening her body to him, which now resulted in a figure made inaccessible by the foreboding mood of a shadow that covers her. She seems sad and remote in her expression, even though the model and the photographer had both come to realize that through their work together they found the only part of their relationship that had remained stable.

Caring little what others thought, Weston allowed himself to incorporate in his photographs a sentiment that he himself might once have thought maudlin. He wrote to Nancy Newhall about two recent nudes of Charis, calling them "pure succotash."[103] In *Winter Idyll* (cat. 56), Charis twirls on a distant swing in what Edward described as a Maxfield Parrish-like setting. This is the kind of image he had criticized years before in the work of others. Other of his photographs were more in tune with the present. *Nude and Blimp* (cat. 57) presents the odd juxtaposition of Charis lounging on a cliffside terrace looking out on the Pacific and a Navy blimp in the distance. As Weston stood back not only from his subject but also from the character of its treatment, he summoned experiences both of his early and recent career. From the early pictorial images, he drew on his photographs of mysterious females posed against shade-shrouded walls in languorous gowns, such as the 1920 *Prologue to a Sad Spring* (fig. 23). As in his recent tableau work, he playfully combined incompatible elements. Now that the war and his own "sad spring" were upon him, he was able to more solemnly recast his past experiences to suit his current situation without a second thought about the sentimentality or surrealistic quality of his subject

(fig. 22 and cat. 57). Perhaps, he wondered if the romantic youth he thought he had lost with the destruction of his earliest daybooks was still a part of the man now struggling to make sense of an irrational world. This curious state of mind, in which creative artists in old age address a former self, allowed Weston to deal with and even embrace his own contradictions, to see and develop what might be called his masculine and feminine sides. As he had experimented with the flat-field composition of the cliffs, Weston, in his last nudes of Charis, seems to have relaxed his photographic habits in order to see what would result from such liberties.

The final break with Charis occurred on November 15, 1945. As a writer, she was confined by having only photography as a subject. She felt trapped as a junior partner to a man twenty-eight years her senior, whose destiny was closing in on him in a way that she could not conceive for herself. She also sensed that she was hurting her husband emotionally: "Edward had begun to sit silently for long periods, and sometimes wouldn't respond even when I spoke to him. . . . His heel would start tapping the floor in what sounded like repressed irritation. . . . It is clear to me now that he was suffering from depression, but in those days we didn't know what that meant; no one considered it a serious medical matter. I feared Edward's moodiness was a reaction to my presence and thought the wisest thing to do was give him some breathing space."[104]

Their friends were crushed to hear the news, for Edward and Charis had seemed a model husband-and-wife team. Their simple lifestyle, dedicated totally to their purposes, had been an inspiration to almost everyone who met them. Nancy Newhall, who shared the same profession with own her husband and understood Charis's predicament, wrote to Edward on November 20: "No—the real shock for those who love you is I think to an ideal to which we have all made pilgrimage—the austere and simple beauty of your life. For recent ones like us it lay on Wildcat Hill and Charis was part of it, and it lay in our hearts like a glow and a challenge to our own frantic and cluttered lives."[105] Adams also knew he would miss the two of them being together, as well as "the little house with the big mood."[106]

Other destinies became apparent that year. Weston was no longer the specimen of health who challenged his sons to sprints and broad jumps. By the time of their marital breakup, his perplex-

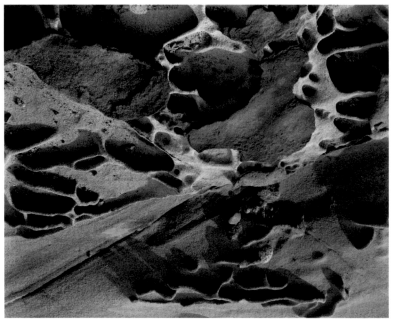

Figure 24. Edward Weston. *Sandstone Erosion, Point Lobos,* 1945 (cat. 66).   Figure 25. Inverted image of fig. 24.

ing muscle tremors, which began with his feet and then extended to his hands, were certainly obvious, even though the diagnosis of Parkinson's disease was not made until long after the Westons' separation and divorce. Always in tune with his health and fastidious about diet, he must have felt something was medically wrong as he began photographing the dark cliffs of Point Lobos, perhaps even earlier.

Weston's two hundred-fifty-print retrospective (with a thirty-six-page catalogue), which opened on February 11, 1946, was the largest one-person exhibition of a photographer's work that the Museum of Modern Art had ever mounted.[107] Although he sold ninety-seven prints and enjoyed excellent reviews, it was not as satisfying for the artist as it would have been had Charis been with him as partner and wife. Weston's professional success continued back in California, when he sold 113 prints of his own choosing to a patron who donated them to the Los Angeles County Museum of Art.[108] This should have been the high point of his career, but the future looked more uncertain than ever.

Even if all else was in confusion, Weston knew he wanted to stay on Wildcat Hill near Point Lobos. After he agreed with Charis on the price of purchasing her half of the property, Edward asked

Cole and his wife if they could move from Los Angeles back to the Carmel area to help him with his new business of publishing books and selling original prints. They arrived in the spring of 1946, and Cole began to photograph with his father for the first time. Even with Cole's enthusiasm and assistance, 1946 was not productive for Edward. The two years following—the last of Weston's active career—were even less so. However, through his irrepressible imagination, the elder Weston found a few new subjects almost as a younger photographer might. One involved placing a small figure in a large landscape, as in his photograph of Brett's daughter, Erica, at Point Lobos (cat. 71). A second was photographing breaking waves against the back-lit effects of the sun (cat. 75), causing them to be dark instead of light. A third was the odd discovery of the reversal of the concave and convex effects of details of eroded sandstone and pebbles if the photograph were turned upside down (see figs. 24–25). These motifs—as well as the many Weston had already made known—would become starting points for Wynn Bullock, Pirkle Jones, Minor White, and scores of other landscape photographers who established themselves from the 1950s on.

The most conspicuous new subject for Weston in 1947 was color. Throughout the year, as Willard Van Dyke focused on him as the subject of what would be an Academy-Award-winning documentary film, *The Photographer*, Weston used color-transparency film. Needing constant help to manipulate the heavy camera and its parts, he took on Dody Thomson as an assistant and student. She had posed for Clarence John Laughlin as a teenager in Louisiana and literally arrived on Edward's doorstep at the very moment Cole and Dorothy had moved down the highway to Garrapata Canyon, and Edward was looking for an extra hand. With Van Dyke and the camera crew, Weston revisited favorite sites such as the cypress root at Point Lobos and Zabriskie Point in Death Valley. The decision to return to well-known places in Weston's career was Van Dyke's, but the idea of using color film in the view camera was prompted by a professional agreement Weston made for promoting the Kodachome and Ektachome products of the Eastman Kodak Company.[109] As he posed for the cinematographer, he was able to think anew about taking color photographs in places he had already conquered in black and white. Although he liked the results enough to publish them under his name as advertisements for Kodak, none came close to matching his latest work at Point Lobos in black and white.

The diminished number of photographs Weston took in the years between 1944 and 1948 does not represent a decline in artistic ability, just opportunity. At the time, White recognized the character of these last works, with their understated, inner emotional dialogues. White, a Weston acolyte who brought his photography classes down from San Francisco to visit the aging photographer, had taken on the position of editor for *Aperture*, a new magazine devoted to photography as an art. In its fourth issue—which appeared in 1953, five years after Weston had to stop taking photographs—White devoted an extended, fourteen-page section to Weston's last photographs of Point Lobos. The brief editor's note is the only text:

> Rarely are we shown the maturest work of men who have lived richly and whose spirit has grown all their lives. This selection was made from the last photographs Edward Weston made at Point Lobos. . . . Lobos is to Weston what the quartette [*sic*] or symphonic form was to Beethoven. In and with this place he has made his most profound statements, the ones closest to his heart. These few pictures may parallel in content the last quartettes of Beethoven, or they may be extraordinary revitalizations of the commonplace.[110]

Three years before the *Aperture* article, Weston, with the aid and encouragement of Ansel and Virginia Adams, had published *My Camera on Point Lobos*, a selection of photographs from throughout his entire career.[111] Of the thirty plates, only three (cats. 60, 65, 76) were from the 1944–48 period. Nevertheless, the book gives a well-rounded sense of Weston's feelings about his favorite place to make photographs. It is one of the few photographic books at that time that, in its selection, sequencing, production, and pensive cover image, constituted an artist's statement. It was not the commercial success that a similar book by Adams, on the more popular subject of Yosemite Valley, had been.[112]

One of the photographs included in the article and the book is a photographic detail of rocks (fig. 26) that was strikingly different from the hundreds Weston had made during his fifteen years on Point Lobos. Spread from edge to edge is a composition of sand and rocks without any perspective depth. Unlike Weston's earlier rock studies, it has no obvious center of interest. Neither was it like his 1944 photographs that display the scar patterns of the dark cliff rocks (see fig. 19). It expresses no obvious psychological mood. There is no sculptural, organic form, no active body of water to be seen. For Dody Thomson, who assisted Weston that day, there was little before the photographer from which to make a decent photograph. What he pictured, however, was something he could feel and see so well: the physical results of forces spent. Weston listed the image in the category of rocks when he assigned it a negative code number, but it does not appear to be a picture just about rocks: it proved to be the last photograph Weston would ever make.

As Thomson has related the story, they were out together at Point Lobos. Again there were two photographers with a difference of lifetimes between them. She was young and vivacious, while he was old and slow. Thomson described Weston as "a smallish, tanned, sturdy-looking man, not particularly handsome, with a ruff of gray hair and a strong nose, but with especially nice eyes . . . exceptionally warm, gay, and penetrating by turns."[113] The patient master, with what she described as "hot brown" eyes, must have been amused by his assistant's anxious search for almost anything on which to try an exposure. Nothing suggested itself. Of course she was avoiding all the many possibilities that Weston's years of hard work had made obvious, as well as what tourists would find engaging. Not much was left,

Figure 26. Edward Weston. *Point Lobos,* 1948 (cat. 76).

it seemed. Weston, however, knew there was a lesson to teach her, even if she did not set up the camera. As she related,

> Edward bet me that we would find something of interest if we merely looked down from our low bluff into the next cove, whatever it might be, and walked over to the edge. But it was just a poor nook of dull, dark sand with a few small, uninteresting rocks scattered about. He stood peering down several seconds. I still saw nothing, but in that time he decided how his finished print would look. With absolute certainty of knowledge and economy of movement he set up the camera and tripod and made preparation. While he measured the light I examined the image on the ground glass at the rear of the camera, under the black sateen cloth which shut out the light, and saw glimmering there, upside down and backwards, a lovely ensemble of silver rocks sailing in pewter sand.[114]

Later, Weston liked to refer to his last photograph as the "Dody Rocks."[115] Perhaps it was a pleasant memory, or just a tease to remind her of the subject that had stared her in the face. Understanding the personal meaning of an image of forces spent

was still beyond her experience. Nevertheless, she learned something profound on that day at Point Lobos. She observed "how technique must become . . . instinctive as breath," and how photographic subjects can be anywhere one needs them to be.[116]

Thomson could not have seen the "Dody Rocks" while she was filled with youth's eagerness to find something worth her film. Weston had learned that, in the end, it is not the film one tries to please, or the public. He had also learned that his goal as an artist was not limited to the capture or control of the subject. What had come to matter most for him was the "meaning of the capture," as Wallace Stevens phrased it.[117] At the age of sixty-two, in this seemingly non-descript photograph, Weston had come to know the meaning of capturing what seemed like nothing to everyone else. Although his health had failed him, his imagination had not.

It had taken Weston a long time to realize that, at Point Lobos and its adjacent coast, he was living in his spiritual home. Jeffers had recognized this instantly and never left, even preparing his deathbed next to a window facing the sea. Stevens expressed the notion of having to search for what in the end seems destined to be. He called it a sense of "unexplained completion," a sense Weston captured in his last photograph, and Stevens in a late work, "The Poem that Took the Place of a Mountain":

> *There it was, word for word,*
> *The poem that took the place of a mountain.*
>
> *He breathed its oxygen,*
> *Even when the book lay turned in the dust of his table.*
>
> *It reminded him how he had needed*
> *A place to go to in his own direction,*
>
> *How he had recomposed the pines,*
> *Shifted the rocks and picked his way among clouds,*
>
> *For the outlook that would be right,*
> *Where he would be complete in an unexplained completion:*

The exact rock where his inexactnesses
Would discover, at last, the view toward which they had edged,

Where he could lie and, gazing down at the sea,
Recognize his unique and solitary home.[118]

Stevens's poem describes Weston, as well as many other artists entering the last period of their careers. Sadly, once Weston recognized the extraordinary power and freedom of old age, he had but a few years to work before an incapacitating illness caught up with him.

On April 22, 1944, Weston had made an entry in his long-neglected daybooks. Knowing, perhaps, that he would not have the time to keep them up, he crammed ten-years'-worth of events in a few pages, mostly listing what happened and remembering the friends who had died. Possibly, Weston considered undertaking another self-examination at this more complex stage of life. He made no other entries, however. Had he maintained the diary through the period of his later work, we might not have to speculate through his photographs, letters, or the memoirs of others why he took the course he did or what he thought about himself. Nonetheless, it seems clear that the self-searching and examination of his life experience that was the cause of those inner dialogues had found their way into his last photographs.

During the final decade of Weston's life, he was inactive as a photographer, but not as a master and host. He welcomed students and admirers every month to his humble home. Many remembered their visits and what they learned from him without his having to teach them directly. Everyone who knew him said he never complained about the debilitating disease that slowly limited his simple movements as well as his fierce independence. Fate had at least spared his mind. It also gave him a last photograph that was meaningful as such, a rare event in the lives of photographers. Even though Weston did not have many years in the final period of old age in which to work, he had crossed its boundary and realized what it meant and what his mission was to himself in that future.

Early on New Year's morning 1958, Weston sat in a chair facing his view of the Pacific Ocean from Wildcat Hill. Whatever he saw was to be his last, private image of the place he had loved and left and to which he always—and ultimately—returned. His sons cremated his body and privately scattered his ashes at Point Lobos on what they called Weston Beach, one of the many places the great master had made his own.[119]

PLATES

In May 1938, Weston moved into a new studio in the Carmel Highlands with his young model, muse, professional partner, and wife-to-be Charis Wilson. He had just completed the most productive year of his career to date. An eleven-month tour of California as a Guggenheim Fellow had provided him with ample opportunity to develop his natural still lifes into more complex compositions of clouds, vistas, and landscape patterns. To break up the routine of printing hundreds of negatives in his new darkroom, he began to revisit nearby Point Lobos, his favorite landscape. For the first time, he photographed the dynamic ocean surf in its various shapes and tones. The fluid forms of rocks and seaweed attracted his eye with new meaning. He also studied sunsets and the values that emerged from summer fogs, two elements that he had once considered too scenic for the modernist photographer he felt himself to be. Suddenly, at the age of fifty-two, Weston found that the world that he had known well seemed new again and his life full of possibilities.

POINT LOBOS, 1938 (cat. 2)

SURF, POINT LOBOS, 1938 (cat. 9)

UNTITLED, 1938 (cat. 13)

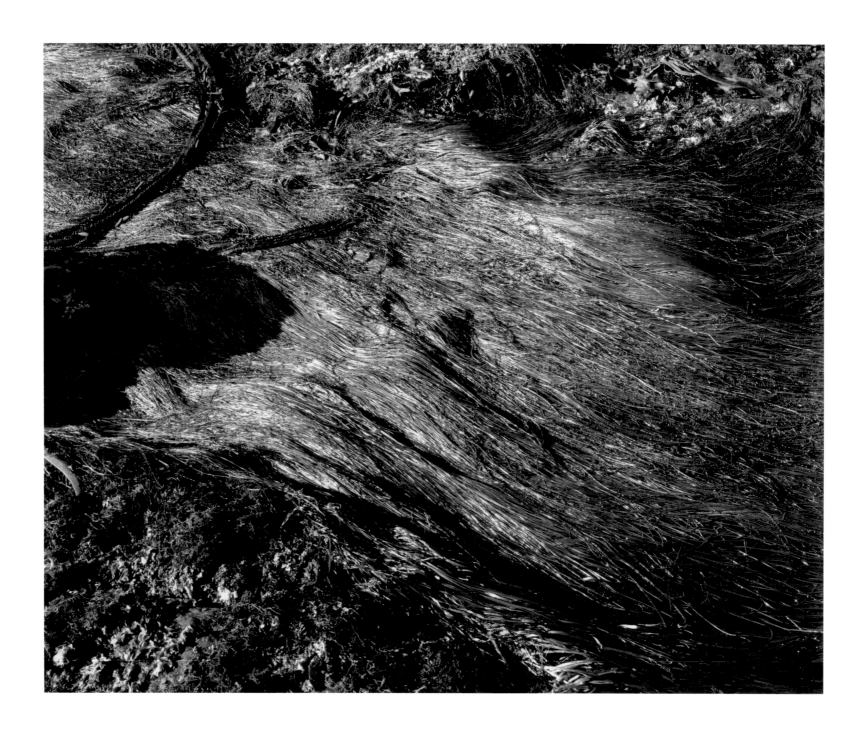

WET SEAWEED, POINT LOBOS, 1938 (cat. 4)

SURF, POINT LOBOS, 1938 (cat. 11)

POINT LOBOS, 1938 (cat. 1)

POINT LOBOS, 1938 (cat. 7)

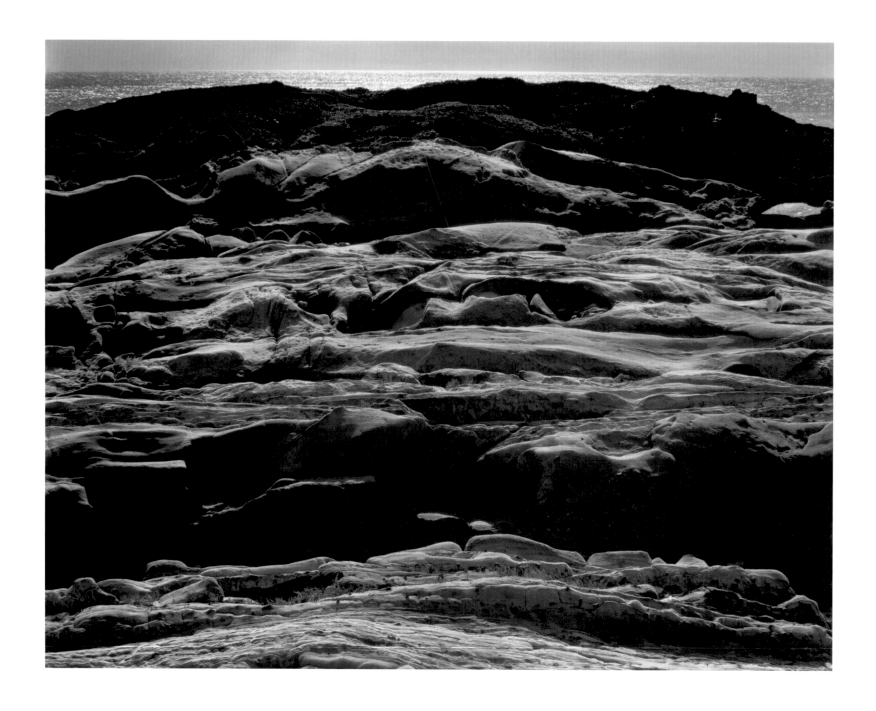

POINT LOBOS, 1939 (cat. 14)

SURF, POINT LOBOS, 1938 (cat. 3)

POINT LOBOS, 1938 (cat. 10)

SURF, POINT LOBOS, 1938 (cat. 12)

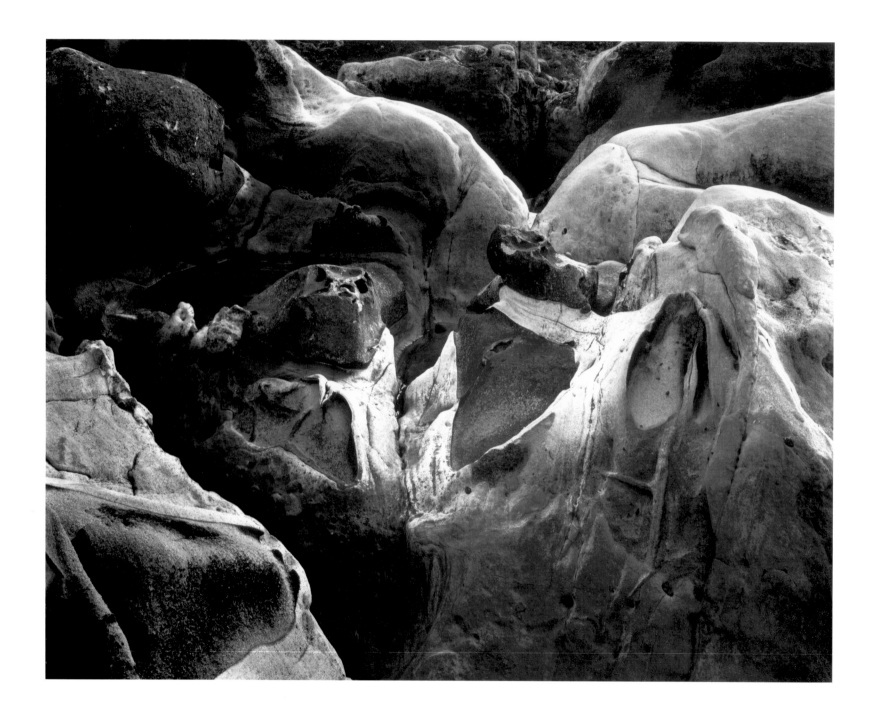

POINT LOBOS, 1938 (cat. 8)

POINT LOBOS, 1939 (cat. 15)

CHINA COVE, POINT LOBOS, 1938 (cat. 6)

FOG AND CYPRESS, POINT LOBOS, 1938 (cat. 5)

One year after his rediscovery of Point Lobos, Weston was not merely recording the objects and atmospheres of the pristine headland in their plain, factual physicality. Increasingly, viewers felt that his photographs suggested moods. They saw the theme of death in what for Weston was a straightforward photograph of Charis floating in her father's swimming pool. Cypress trees and tide-pool rocks struck some as painful, tortured shapes, and the tonality of a calm sea state after a storm as sad. In addition to such psychological readings, Weston's photographs in 1939 and 1940 begin to reveal a new level of compositional sophistication. The presentation within a single frame of masculine and feminine elements, oppositions of light and dark, and symbols of life and death enriched his photography. The metaphorical potential of Weston's work during World War II and after allows even the most abstract still lifes to appear as scarred battlefields, and sandstone erosions as disoriented characters. The photographer stated, however, that he never intended such meanings. Nonetheless, as he developed beyond technical virtuosity, Weston was capable of creating photographs that could hold more profound meanings, and thus a greater variety of interpretations.

NUDE FLOATING, 1939 (cat. 19)

GLASS AND LILY, 1939 (cat. 18)

KELP, POINT LOBOS, 1939 (cat. 16)

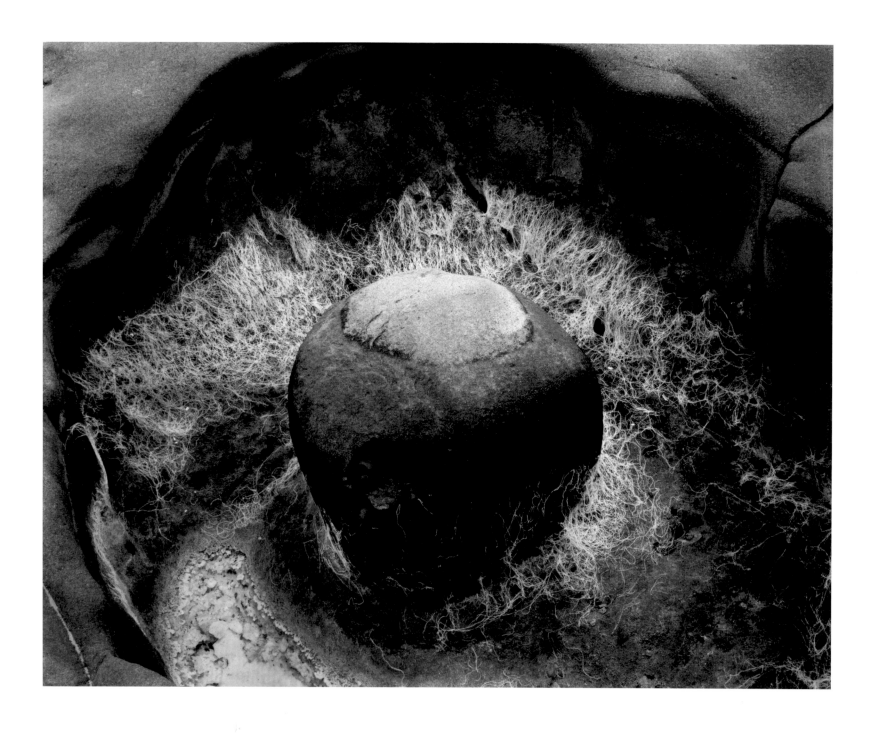

DRY TIDE POOL, POINT LOBOS, 1939 (cat. 17)

CYPRESS, POINT LOBOS, 1940 (cat. 22)

SAN SIMEON HIGHWAY, 1940 (cat. 23)

SEA, POINT LOBOS, 1940 (cat. 21)

CHINA COVE, POINT LOBOS, 1940 (cat. 20)

POINT LOBOS, 1941 (cat. 24)

DEAD PELICAN, POINT LOBOS, 1942 (cat. 27)

STONECROP AND CYPRESS, POINT LOBOS, 1941 (cat. 25)

TAR DRIPPINGS, POINT LOBOS, 1942 (cat. 29)

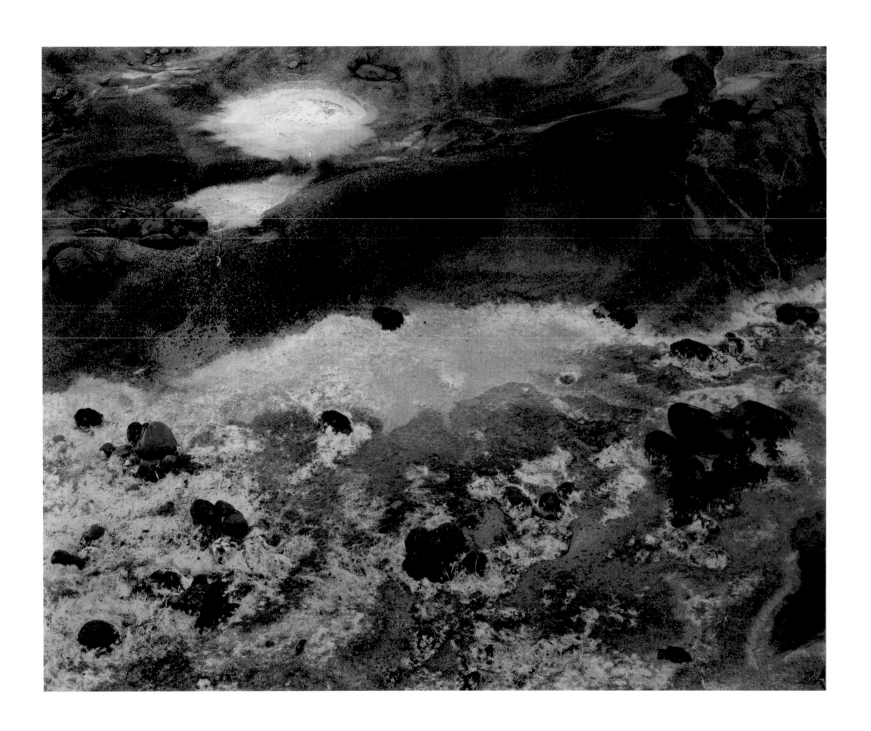

SALT-ENCRUSTED ROCK, POINT LOBOS, 1942 (cat. 30)

SANDSTONE EROSION, POINT LOBOS, 1945 (cat. 66)

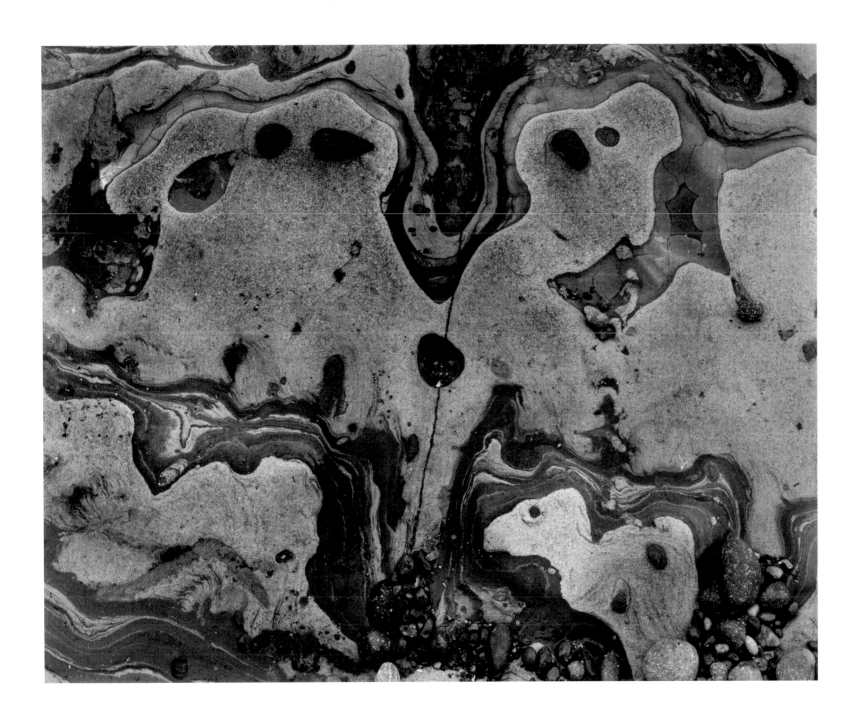

ERODED ROCK, POINT LOBOS, 1942 (cat. 28)

The war years were frustrating ones for Weston as an artist. Point Lobos was closed to civilians for the first part of this period, and gas rationing restricted the travel he had become accustomed to on his Guggenheim Fellowships (1937–39) and his 1941 commission to illustrate Walt Whitman's *Leaves of Grass*. He and Charis became airplane spotters and tended their victory garden on Wildcat Hill. What little photography he did was restricted to his own property or that of friends. He responded to what presented itself—Charis coming home with her first gas mask—or what he could instigate— friends and relatives posing for satiric tableaux. The artificiality of these works did not bother Weston as much as they did his friends, who thought they knew what to expect of the photographer. Weston also began to photograph the many cats he and Charis kept around the studio as illustrations for a book she was writing. Through the cat book and composing tableaux, the Westons shared some happy hours in a marriage that was becoming more uncertain with every passing year.

CIVILIAN DEFENSE, 1942 (cat. 26)

MY LITTLE GRAY HOME IN THE WEST, 1943 (cat. 37)

GOOD NEIGHBOR POLICY, 1943 (cat. 36)

EXPOSITION OF DYNAMIC SYMMETRY, 1943 (cat. 38)

CHARIS AND MARCO POLO, 1945 (cat. 59)

CATS ON WOODBOX, 1944 (cat. 39)

NUDE, 1943 (cat. 35)

During the war, Weston looked more closely at his domestic life. His backyard set-ups and the portraits of his cats could be considered diversions when compared to the work he had done and had hoped to do in landscape. Although he had pursued landscape subjects almost exclusively during the previous five years, he remained a talented, professional portrait photographer. Weston could compliment paying customers with his skills of photographic flattery and still satisfy himself in portraits of his artistic and intellectual associates. When he turned his attention to his immediate family, he wanted to escape the formality of the studio and its lighting. Using both his professional experience and the skills he had developed from dealing with the changing conditions of landscape photography, Weston created some of the most beautiful portraits of his career. Unlike the backyard tableaux, the portraits of his sons and their families contain his personal feelings of caring and concern. Weston saw his sons not only living life on their own as men, husbands, and fathers, but as the primary source of his own emotional stability in difficult times.

PORTRAIT OF COLE WESTON AND HIS WIFE, DOROTHY, 1945 (cat. 53)

COLE, 1942 (cat. 32)

CHAN AND TED, 1944 (cat. 50)

PORTRAIT OF NEIL WESTON, 1943 (cat. 34)

NEIL, 1942 (cat. 33)

BRETT AND ERICA, 1944 (cat. 51)

BRETT AND ERICA, 1945 (cat. 52)

In 1944, at the age of fifty-eight, Weston took a series of landscapes at Point Lobos that more consistently reflect the mood of his private life than any he had made before. His marriage was dissolving; his sons joining the navy, army, and merchant marines; and he may have been experiencing the first tremors of Parkinson's disease. In these pictures, Weston occasionally allowed the cliffsides to spread out beyond the tight control of his habitual framing. The viewer's eye thus wanders more freely and, in the darker tones, more pensively. Here, the quiet lamentation of an accepted fate, rather than the lively celebration of a newly conquered world, seems to determine the resulting character. These photographs would prove to be some of the most meaningful of his late career. They parallel the German poet Rainer Maria Rilke's description of hours of pain and nights of anguish in the tenth of his *Duino Elegies*: "one season in our inner year—, not only a season / in time—, but . . . place and settlement, foundation and soil and home."

POINT LOBOS, 1944 (cat. 44)

POINT LOBOS, 1944 (cat. 42)

CLIFF AND STONECROP, 1944 (cat. 41)

SANDSTONE EROSION, POINT LOBOS, 1945 (cat. 67)

POINT LOBOS, 1944 (cat. 48)

DRIED KELP AND DRIFTWOOD, POINT LOBOS, 1944 (cat. 40)

CYPRESS, POINT LOBOS, 1944 (cat. 49)

POINT LOBOS, 1944 (cat. 46)

STONECROP, POINT LOBOS, 1944 (cat. 47)

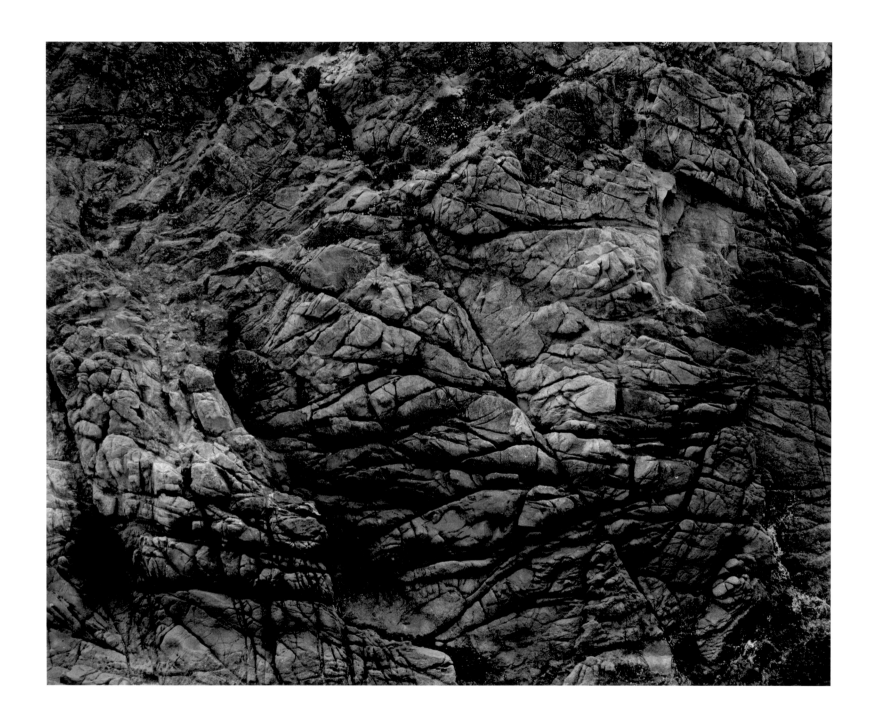

GRANITE CLIFF, POINT LOBOS, 1944 (cat. 45)

GRANITE CLIFF, POINT LOBOS, 1946 (cat. 69)

The few nudes of his wife that Weston took at the beginning of
the war were playful demonstrations of the futility of meaning.
A lounging nude in a gas mask with a frond of a fern added merely
for compositional balance is an image of stray and misleading clues
available for almost any interpretation. The nudes of Charis from
1945 tell a different story. Their marriage had only a measure of
months before it would end, in mid-November. During the course
of the year, Weston no longer saw his subject through one particular
temperament or style. He employed different aesthetic strategies for
different situations: modernist geometry, atmospheric sentimentality,
and surrealistic juxtaposition. One reason for this change may be
that, like other great artists entering old age, Weston chose to please
no one but himself and availed himself of the enormous freedom
that such an approach permits. As the images reveal, model and
photographer still cooperated with each other in making photographs, but remained in separate and distant emotional worlds. The
results from such a disjunctive situation are, however, inexplicably
stunning and subtle.

NUDE, 1945 (cat. 55)

NUDE, 1945 (cat. 54)

WINTER IDYLL, 1945 (cat. 56)

NUDE, 1945 (cat. 58)

NUDE AND BLIMP, 1945 (cat. 57)

7 A.M. PACIFIC WAR TIME, 1945 (cat. 61)

HEIMY, 1945 (cat. 62)

After 1945 the slow but steady progression of Parkinson's disease kept Weston from making as many photographs as he would have liked. Increasingly, he needed help just to manage his heavy view camera and equipment. His sons came to his assistance, as did other younger photographers and friends. Although his pace had slowed, his imagination was as active as ever. Through his genius, he triumphed over his afflictions and created new, almost contradictory, approaches to taking photographs. If some of his works address death and chaos, others speak of life and composure. If a few display the active and spectacular forces of light and water, others ponder the shape and residue of forces spent. In 1948 Weston exposed his last negative, a profoundly enigmatic and beautiful image of rocks scattered on a beach at Point Lobos (cat. 76). Although the photograph was not intended to be a final statement, it is perhaps an appropriate ending image for his long career. In the decade leading up to his last photograph, Weston had come to see life not just as the exhilaration of a moment, but as a complicated cycle replete with mysteries and resolutions.

DEAD PELICAN, POINT LOBOS, 1945 (cat. 60)

POINT LOBOS, 1946 (cat. 68)

NORTH DOME, POINT LOBOS, 1946 (cat. 64)

FLOATING DRIFTWOOD, 1945 (cat. 63)

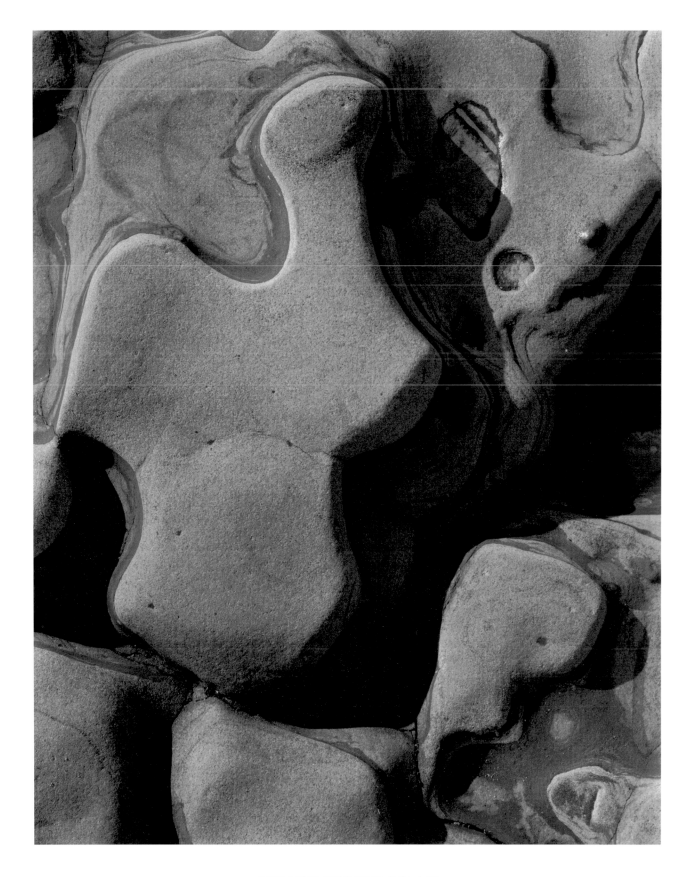

ERODED ROCK, POINT LOBOS, 1946 (cat. 70)

POINT LOBOS, 1946 (cat. 65)

ERICA, POINT LOBOS, 1947 (cat. 71)

UNTITLED, 1947 (cat. 72)

POINT LOBOS, 1947 (cat. 75)

POINT LOBOS, 1947 (cat. 73)

UNTITLED, 1947 (cat. 74)

POINT LOBOS, 1948 (cat. 76)

A book that deals with an artist's life and the emotional circumstances associated with his work cannot claim to have any semblance of accuracy without direct input from those who lived alongside him. I am deeply indebted to Edward Weston's second wife, Charis Wilson, for her patient assistance and thoughtful suggestions not only as I formed my ideas but after I completed the first drafts of my text. Her daughter Rachel Harris was also of enormous help in correcting my essay and assisting her mother. Edward Weston's youngest son, Cole, was indispensable in helping me to achieve an accurate portrait of the father he loved and assisted through many difficult years of declining health. A highly accomplished photographer himself, Cole immediately understood my quest to understand the origin of both the famous and obscure photographs his father made in his great, final years. The book Cole's wife Paulette prepared of the correspondence between father and son proved an essential resource

A remarkable group of people who are part of the Weston family provided valuable assistance. Margaret Weston of the Weston Gallery in Carmel was ever supportive of my efforts. The photographer's grandson Kim Weston, a fine photographer in his own right, and his wife, Gina, generously acted as my personal guides to the famous Weston home and studio on Wildcat Hill, where they now live.

A number of colleagues in the field were extremely helpful on a number of fronts. Rita Bottoms, Head of Special Collections at the Library of the University of California, Santa Cruz, made the archive of Weston's project prints available to me without restriction and arranged for a substantial number of loans to the exhibition. She was a constant source of information and leads to other resources. I am grateful to her cordial staff, Carol Champion and Paul Stubbs. The administration and staff of the Center for Creative

ACKNOWLEDGMENTS

to gauge the depth of Weston's thoughts in his later years, after he had ceased making entries in his daybooks.

Dr. Amy Conger, the indisputable expert on Weston's career, spent many hours reviewing my writing and leading me to facts and photographs that support my thesis. Her catalogue of Weston's archive has become the bible of every Weston scholar; I am indebted to that study, as well as to her many published articles and catalogues.

Those who knew Weston intimately as friend, teacher, or colleague contributed unselfishly to my research. Chief among them is Dody Warren Thompson, Weston's last photographic assistant and daughter-in-law, through her marriage to his son Brett. The memories and writing of Ruth-Marion Baruch also inspired me. She understood Weston as one of his last models and a photographic colleague, and also as a scholar who wrote the first master's dissertation on his work. Her husband, Pirle Jones, another remarkable photographic talent and friend of Weston, was extremely generous with his time, hospitality, and insight as well. I owe a special debt of gratitude to Rose Mandel, also a student-colleague of Weston in his last years. A photographer and student of psychology, she, more than anyone I have met, understands the essential connection between the inner mind of artists and the expression of their talents.

Photography at the University of Arizona, Tucson, were invaluable in my research and as lenders to the exhibition. In particular I thank Terrence Pitts, former Director, and Nancy Lutz, former Deputy Director, as well as Trudy Wilner Stack, Dianne Nilsen, and Amy Rule. I am also grateful to Saundra B. Lane, Karen Haas, and Karen Quinn of the Lane Collection for their support.

The one resource that keeps a writer from muddled prose and foolishness is a battery of readers. Anstiss Hammond Krueck; Ralph and Helen Mills; Elizabeth Siegel; my wife, Leslie Travis; and William A. Turnage kept me on a clear track of explanation. I remember with special pleasure many stimulating conversations about artistic ideas and the unique condition of old age with both young and experienced artists and scholars, including Tom Bamberger; David Hartt; Sandra Sammataro Phillips, Curator of Photography at the San Francisco Museum of Modern Art; Irene Siegel; and John Szarkowski.

Without the talented and experienced team who produced this book, few of my ideas and none of Weston's later photographs would have had the beautiful presentation they enjoy here. Encouraging me at every step was the book's editor, Susan F. Rossen, Executive Director of Publications at The Art Institute of Chicago. Karen Altschul served as photo editor. Greg Nosan proofed the manuscript. Amanda Freymann employed her extensive experience, particularly in photographic-book production, to find solutions to my many requests for special treatment of the images and the design of the book. Robert Hennessey applied his exacting standards to capture the delicate, dark feeling and quality that Weston's later prints contain. He worked with Alan Newman and Greg Williams of the Art Institute's Imaging Department, who were responsible for the digital scans. Registrarial duties were handled by Martha C. Sharma. Dorothy Schroeder, Assistant to the Director, kept the administration and the budget of the project tangle-free. I am grateful for the high professionalism of those members of my staff who worked on the exhibition: Lisa D'Acquisto, James Iska, Kristin Merrill, Sylvie Penichon, and Douglas Severson. Graphic designer Jody Hanson's devotion to balance, clarity, and grace in the imposition of type and image on the printed page resulted in a book that the exacting Weston would have admired.

This exhibition and catalogue would not have begun without Bill Hood, Managing Director of Corporate Affairs, of American Airlines, who is not only a photography enthusiast but, for many years, has been a guiding source of inspiration and support, through numerous major exhibitions and publications in the Department of Photography. Nicholas J. Pritzker, John Burlingame, and Larry Schulman of the Hyatt Development Corporation and the Hyatt Vacation Club have also been instrumental in supporting this publication.

Last, but not least, I am grateful to James N. Wood, Director and President of the Art Institute, for his encouragement in my pursuit of understanding the genius of great photographers and particularly the condition that age and experience add to the depth and flavor of great work.

David Travis

Editor's Note

All works are gelatin silver prints; height precedes width. Weston numbers are those the photographer assigned to his negatives during his lifetime. Conger numbers refer to entries in Amy Conger, *Edward Weston Photographs from the Collection of the Center for Creative Photography* (Tucson, 1992). This source also explains, in Appendix A, Weston's negative numbering system. Brett Weston printed the photographs from the University of California, Santa Cruz, in 1954 under his father's direction, as he did the photographs from The Art Institute of Chicago accessioned in 1959. Prints made toward the end of Weston's career are difficult to assign to a specific printer, as his sons assisted him in the darkroom and printed from his negatives after his death. Weston probably printed cats. 13, 24, 36, 42, 46–47, 55, and 58–59.

6. *China Cove, Point Lobos*, 1938
19.4 x 24.5 cm
University of California, Santa Cruz, UCSC 560
Weston PL–L–23g   Conger 1362
Plate p. 68

7. *Point Lobos*, 1938
The Art Institute of Chicago, gift of Max McGraw, 1959.761
19.3 x 24.4 cm
Weston PL–R–20g   Conger 1364
Plate p. 61

8. *Point Lobos*, 1938
19.2 x 24.4 cm
The Art Institute of Chicago, gift of Max McGraw, 1959.775
Weston PL–R–21g   Conger 1365
Plate p. 66

9. *Surf, Point Lobos*, 1938
19.4 x 24.4 cm
The Art Institute of Chicago, gift of Max McGraw, 1959.78
Weston PL–S–9g   Conger 1367
Plate p. 56

15. *Point Lobos*, 1939
24.4 x 19.4 cm
University of California, Santa Cruz, UCSC 639
Weston PL 39–MI–5   Conger 1474
Plate p. 67

16. *Kelp, Point Lobos*, 1939
19.3 x 24.3 cm
The Art Institute of Chicago, gift of Max McGraw, 1959.793
Weston PL 39–P–2   Conger 1490
Plate p. 73

17. *Dry Tide Pool, Point Lobos*, 1939
19.4 x 24.4 cm
University of California, Santa Cruz, UCSC 636
Weston PL 39–R–1   Conger 1493
Plate p. 74

18. *Glass and Lily*, 1939
19.3 x 24.5 cm
University of California, Santa Cruz, UCSC 660
Weston C 39–MI–1   Conger 1497
Plate p. 72

CHECKLIST

1. *Point Lobos*, 1938
19.2 x 24.4 cm
University of California, Santa Cruz, UCSC 545
Weston PL–L–7g   Conger 1347
Plate p. 60; figure 8 p. 26

2. *Point Lobos*, 1938
19.1 x 24.3 cm
The Art Institute of Chicago, gift of Max McGraw, 1959.771
Weston PL–L–8g   Conger 1349
Plate p. 55

3. *Surf, Point Lobos*, 1938
19.1 x 24.4 cm
The Art Institute of Chicago, gift of Max McGraw, 1959.777
Weston PL–S–3g   Conger 1355
Plate p. 63

4. *Wet Seaweed, Point Lobos*, 1938
19.5 x 24.3 cm
University of California, Santa Cruz, UCSC 563
Weston PL–K–3g   Conger 1357
Plate p. 58

5. *Fog and Cypress, Point Lobos*, 1938
19.4 x 24.3 cm
University of California, Santa Cruz, UCSC 558
Weston PL–L–10g   Conger 1359
Plate p. 69

10. *Point Lobos*, 1938
The Art Institute of Chicago, gift of Max McGraw, 1959.764
19.5 x 24.3 cm
Weston PL–L–18g   Conger 1368
Plate p. 64; cover

11. *Surf, Point Lobos*, 1938
19.3 x 24.4 cm
The Art Institute of Chicago, gift of Max McGraw, 1959.749
Weston PL–S–14g   Conger 1370
Plate p. 59

12. *Surf, Point Lobos*, 1938
19.1 x 24.4 cm
The Art Institute of Chicago, gift of Max McGraw, 1959.750
Weston PL–S–17g   Conger 1373
Plate p. 65

13. *Untitled*, 1938
19.2 x 24.5 cm
University of Arizona, Tucson, 81:251:005
Conger 1375
Plate p. 57; figure 9 p. 26

14. *Point Lobos*, 1939
18.8 x 24.3 cm
The Art Institute of Chicago, gift of Max McGraw, 1959.798
Weston PL–R–25g   Conger 1443
Plate p. 62

19. *Nude Floating*, 1939
24 x 24.5 cm
University of California, Santa Cruz, UCSC 670
Weston N 39–C–2   Conger 1500
Plate p. 71

20. *China Cove, Point Lobos*, 1940
24.2 x 19.4 cm
The Art Institute of Chicago, gift of Max McGraw, 1959.802
Weston PL 40–K–4   Conger 1530
Plate p. 78

21. *Sea, Point Lobos*, 1940
24 x 24. 4 cm
University of California, Santa Cruz, UCSC 683
Weston PL 40–S–3   Conger 1534
Plate p. 77

22. *Cypress, Point Lobos*, 1940
19.4 x 24.4 cm
University of California, Santa Cruz, UCSC 685
Weston PL 40–T–3   Conger 1537
Plate p. 75

23. *San Simeon Highway*, 1940
19.3 x 24.0 cm
The Art Institute of Chicago, gift of Max McGraw, 1959.803
Weston SSH–S–3   Conger 1541
Plate p. 76

24. *Point Lobos*, 1941
19.2 x 24.3 cm
University of Arizona, Tucson, 81:208:048
PL 41–MI–1   Conger 1542
Plate p. 79

25. *Stonecrop and Cypress, Point Lobos*, 1941
19.3 x 24.4 cm
University of California, Santa Cruz, UCSC 688
Weston PL 41–T–1   Conger 1545
Plate p. 81

26. *Civilian Defense*, 1942
19.3 x 24.3 cm
The Art Institute of Chicago, gift of Max McGraw, 1959.829
Weston N 42–C–1
Plate p. 87

27. *Dead Pelican, Point Lobos*, 1942
19.3 x 24.3 cm
University of California, Santa Cruz, UCSC 770
Weston PL 42–BI–1   Conger 1696
Plate p. 80; figure 20 p. 45

28. *Eroded Rock, Point Lobos*, 1942
19.2 x 24.2 cm
The Art Institute of Chicago, gift of Max McGraw, 1959.818
Weston PL 42–R–2x   Conger 1702
Plate p. 85

29. *Tar Drippings, Point Lobos*, 1942
19.4 x 24.4 cm
University of California, Santa Cruz, UCSC 767
Weston PL 42–R–3x   Conger 1704
Plate p. 82

30. *Salt–encrusted Rock, Point Lobos*, 1942
19.3 x 24.3 cm
The Art Institute of Chicago, gift of Max McGraw, 1959.817
Weston PL 42–R–4   Conger 1706
Plate p. 83; figure 14 p. 39

31. *Wildcat Hill*, 1942
17 x 24.1 cm
The Art Institute of Chicago, restricted gift of Lucia Woods
Lindley and Daniel A. Lindley, Jr.
Weston C 42–WCH–1   Conger 1712
Figure 7 p. 25

32. *Cole*, 1942
19.5 x 24.3 cm
University of California, Santa Cruz, UCSC 773
Weston PO 42–C–1   Conger 1713
Plate p. 96

33. *Neil*, 1942
19.4 x 24.2 cm
University of California, Santa Cruz, UCSC 772
Weston PO 42–N–1   Conger 1715
Plate p. 99; figure 17 p. 40

34. *Portrait of Neil Weston*, 1943
24.2 x 19.2 cm
The Art Institute of Chicago, restricted gift of Mrs. Everett
Kovler, 1964.132
Weston PO 43–N–2
Plate p. 98

35. *Nude*, 1943
19.2 x 24.3 cm
The Art Institute of Chicago, gift of Max McGraw, 1959.83
Weston N 43–CH–1   Conger 1720
Plate p. 93

36. *Good Neighbor Policy*, 1943
24.3 x 19.3 cm
University of Arizona, Tucson, 81:110:141
Weston SL 43–C–4   Conger 1721
Plate p. 89

37. *My Little Gray Home in the West*, 1943
24.2 x 19.3 cm
The Art Institute of Chicago, gift of Max McGraw, 1959.831
Weston N 43–CH&L–2   Conger 1722
Plate p. 88

38. *Exposition of Dynamic Symmetry*, 1943
19.2 x 24.3 cm
The Art Institute of Chicago, gift of Max McGraw, 1959.832
Weston PO 43–CNLJ–1   Conger 1724
Plate p. 90

39. *Cats on Woodbox*, 1944
19.4 x 24.4 cm
The Art Institute of Chicago, gift of Max McGraw, 1959.835
Weston C 44–CTS–23   Conger 1740
Plate p. 92

40. *Dried Kelp and Driftwood, Point Lobos*, 1944
24.5 x 19.3 cm
University of California, Santa Cruz, UCSC 791
Weston PL 44–K–1   Conger 1746
Plate p. 108

41. *Cliff and Stonecrop*, 1944
19.5 x 24.4 cm
University of California, Santa Cruz, UCSC 787
Weston PL 44–L–1   Conger 1747
Plate p. 105

42. *Point Lobos*, 1944
19.3 x 24.4 cm
University of Arizona, Tucson, 81:110:082
Weston PL 44–3   Conger 1748
Plate p. 104

43. *Point Lobos*, 1944
19.3 x 24.3 cm
The Art Institute of Chicago, gift of Max McGraw, 1959.833
Weston PL 44–L–2   Conger 1749
Frontispiece p. 2

44. *Point Lobos*, 1944
19.4 x 24.6 cm
University of California, Santa Cruz, UCSC 789
Weston PL 44–L–4   Conger 1750
Plate p. 103

45. *Granite Cliff, Point Lobos*, 1944
19.4 x 24.4 cm
University of California, Santa Cruz, UCSC 793
Weston PL 44–R–6   Conger 1752
Plate p. 112; figure 19 p. 44

46. *Point Lobos*, 1944
19.3 x 24.4 cm
University of Arizona, Tucson, 81:208:076
Weston PL 44–R–3   Conger 1754
Plate p. 110

47. *Stonecrop, Point Lobos*, 1944
19.1 x 24.4 cm
University of Arizona, Tucson, 81:110:138
Weston PL 44–R–10   Conger 1755
Plate p. 111

48. *Point Lobos*, 1944
19.4 x 24.6 cm
University of California, Santa Cruz, UCSC 792
Weston PL 44–R–5   Conger 1756
Plate p. 107

49. *Cypress, Point Lobos*, 1944
19.4 x 24.4 cm
University of California, Santa Cruz, UCSC 790
Weston PL 44–T–1   Conger 1759
Plate p. 109

50. *Chan and Ted*, 1944
19 x 24.1 cm
University of California, Santa Cruz, UCSC 776
Weston PO 44–C&T–3   Conger 1766
Plate p. 97

51. *Brett and Erica*, 1944
19.2 x 24.5 cm
University of California, Santa Cruz, UCSC 777
Weston PO 44–B&E–1   Conger 1767
Plate p. 100

52. *Brett and Erica*, 1945
23.9 x 18.8 cm
University of California, Santa Cruz, UCSC 778
Weston PO 45–B&E–1   Conger 1768
Plate p. 101

53. *Portrait of Cole Weston and His Wife, Dorothy*, 1945
19.3 x 24.2 cm
The Art Institute of Chicago, restricted gift of Mrs. Everett
Kovler, 1964.135
Weston PO 45–C&D–1
Plate p. 95

54. *Nude*, 1945
19.3 x 24.5 cm
University of California, Santa Cruz, UCSC 784
Weston N 45–C–1   Conger 1769
Plate p. 116; figure 22 p. 46

55. *Nude*, 1945
19.1 x 24.3 cm
University of Arizona, Tucson, 81:275:014
Weston N 45–CH–5   Conger 1771
Plate p. 115

56. *Winter Idyll*, 1945
19.4 x 24.3 cm
University of California, Santa Cruz, UCSC 785
Weston N 45–C–2   Conger 1772
Plate p. 117

57. *Nude and Blimp*, 1945
19.2 x 24.3 cm
University of Arizona, Tucson, 81:110:002
Weston N 45–CH–4   Conger 1773
Plate p. 119

58. *Nude*, 1945
24.4 x 19.3 cm
William H. Lane Collection
Weston N 45–CH–8
Plate p. 118

59. *Charis and Marco Polo*, 1945
19.4 x 24.4 cm
William H. Lane Collection
Weston C 45–CTS–8
Plate p. 91

60. *Dead Pelican, Point Lobos*, 1945
19 x 21.7 cm
The Art Institute of Chicago, gift of Max McGraw, 1959.838
Weston PL 45–BI–1   Conger 1782
Plate p. 123; figure 21 p. 45

61. *7 a.m. Pacific War Time*, 1945
19.2 x 24.2 cm
The Art Institute of Chicago, gift of Max McGraw, 1959.839
Weston C 45–FOG–1   Conger 1792
Plate p. 120

62. *Heimy*, 1945
19.1 x 24.3 cm
Posthumous reproduction print
University of Arizona, Tucson
Weston N 45–CH–6   Conger 1795
Plate p. 121

63. *Floating Driftwood*, 1945
19.1 x 24 cm
University of Arizona, Tucson, 81:110:139
Weston PL 45–P–1   Conger 1796
Plate p. 126

64. *North Dome, Point Lobos*, 1946
24.1 x 19.2 cm
The Art Institute of Chicago, Peabody Fund, 1952.223
Weston PL 46–L–1   Conger 1806
Plate p. 125; figure 2 p. 13

65. *Point Lobos*, 1946
24.3 x 19.2 cm
The Art Institute of Chicago, gift of Max McGraw, 1959.842
Weston PL 46–L–2   Conger 1807
Plate p. 128

66. *Sandstone Erosion, Point Lobos*, 1945
19.3 x 24.4 cm
University of Arizona, Tucson, 81:110:087
Weston PL45–R–2   Conger 1798
Plate p. 84; figures 24–25, p. 48

67. *Sandstone Erosion, Point Lobos*, 1945
19.4 x 24.4 cm
University of California, Santa Cruz, UCSC 819
Weston PL 45–R–3
Plate p. 106

68. *Point Lobos*, 1946
24.3 x 19.1 cm
University of California, Santa Cruz, UCSC 824
Weston PL46–L–4   Conger 1809
Plate p. 124

69. *Granite Cliff, Point Lobos*, 1946
19.3 x 24.4 cm
University of California, Santa Cruz, UCSC 825
Weston PL 46–R–1   Conger 1810
Plate p. 113

70. *Eroded Rock, Point Lobos*, 1946
24.2 x 19.3 cm
The Art Institute of Chicago, gift of Max McGraw, 1959.841
Weston PL 46–R–2   Conger 1811
Plate p. 127

71. *Erica, Point Lobos*, 1947
19.4 x 25.3 cm
University of California, Santa Cruz, UCSC 829
Weston PL 47–ER–1   Conger 1816
Plate p. 129

72. *Untitled*, 1947
24.2 x 19.3 cm
University of Arizona, Tucson, 81:208:057
Weston PL 47–L–1   Conger 1817
Plate p. 130

73. *Point Lobos*, 1947
19.4 x 24.3 cm
The Art Institute of Chicago, gift of Max McGraw, 1959.843
Weston PL 47–R–1   Conger 1820
Plate p. 132

74. *Untitled*, 1947
24.2 x 19.2 cm
University of Arizona, Tucson, 81:208:078
Weston PL 47–R–2   Conger 1821
Plate p. 133

75. *Point Lobos*, 1947
19.3 x 24.3 cm
The Art Institute of Chicago, gift of Max McGraw, 1959.808
Weston PL 47–S–1   Conger 1822
Plate p. 131

76. *Point Lobos*, 1948
19.5 x 24.2 cm
The Art Institute of Chicago, gift of Max McGraw, 1959.844
Weston Pl 48–R–1   Conger 1826
Plate p. 135; figure 26 p. 50

1. William Butler Yeats, "The Tower" (1928), in *The Collected Poems of W. B. Yeats* (New York, 1956), p. 192.

2. Quoted in Cole Weston, "Edward Weston Dedicated to Simplicity," in Thomas Buchsteiner, *Edward, Cole, Kim Weston: Three Generations of American Photography* (Kilchberg/Zurich, 1989), p. 10.

3. The history of the name is discussed in Donald Thomas Clark, *Monterey County Place Names: A Geographical Dictionary* (Carmel Valley, Calif., 1991), pp. 407–408: "As a map name, Point Lobos goes back, at least, to 1823, when José Narvaez called it *Punta de Lovos*. In 1839 it is shown on a diseño of Rancho San Jose y Sur Chiquito as *Punta de Lobos*." Most authorities agree that the Spanish term *lobos* derives from the plural of *lobo marino* (seal or sea lion). Only since 1890 has Point Lobos been applied to the entire cape; this designation was made permanent in 1933 by the creation of Point Lobos State Reserve.

4. Weston (note 2).

5. After Weston coined the term "prevision," Minor White popularized "previsualization" to describe how an experienced photographer can scan a scene before the camera or inspect an image on the ground glass and "see" the tonal renditions that will characterize the final print. White was in Weston's circle of adulators when he was living in the Bay Area in the late 1940s and early 1950s.

6. In 1915 Weston traveled north from his modest portrait studio in a quiet suburb of Los Angeles (then Tropico, now Glendale) to visit the Pan-Pacific Exposition in San Francisco, where some of his photographs were on view.

7. Hagemeyer met Weston in Los Angeles in 1917, immediately after the former's interest in photography had brought him into contact with Alfred Stieglitz and his circle in New York. For a year, Hagemeyer, who had trained as a horticulturist, took up residence with the Westons while finding his way into the new profession, earning his keep by cleaning the portrait studio and the house. During the early part of his career, Hagemeyer's unanchored lifestyle and interest in anarchism kept him on the move; he never lived more than two years in a single location.

8. When the stock market crashed in the fall of 1929, Hagemeyer, who had ended up in Pasadena, had to return to Carmel and San Francisco, forcing Weston to rent other lodgings.

9. Edward Weston, *Daybooks* (New York, 1966), ed. Nancy Newhall, vol. 2, p. 95.

10. Ibid., pp. 110-11.

11. Ibid., p. 114. The art director and book designer Merle Armitage was a close friend of Weston. As an entrepreneurial publisher, he was responsible for the issue of Weston's first monograph, *The Art of Edward Weston* (New York, 1932), which included thirty-nine reproductions and texts by Armitage, Jean Charlot, Arthur Millier, Lincoln Steffens, and Weston. He undertook other publishing efforts for Weston and remained a patron and promoter of his work throughout the photographer's life.

12. Robinson Jeffers, "Credo" (1927), in *Rock and Hawk: A Selection of Shorter Poems by Robinson Jeffers*, ed. Robert Hass (New York, 1987), p. 67.

13. Weston (note 9), vol. 2, p. 125.

14. Quoted in Harold and Ann Gilliam, *Creating Carmel: The Enduring Vision*, 2d ed. (Salt Lake City, 1996), p. 70.

15. Arnold Genthe, *As I Remember* (New York, 1936), p. 59.

16. Charis Wilson with Wendy Madar, *Through Another Lens: My Years with Edward Weston* (New York, 1998), p. 20.

17. Quoted in James Karman, *Robinson Jeffers: Poet of California* (San Francisco, 1987), p. 78.

18. Quoted in Gilliam (note 14), p. 6.

19. Corinne L. Gilb, "Johan Hagemeyer, Photographer," transcript of tape recorded on Jan. 23, 1956, for the Regional Cultural History Project, Library, University of California, Berkeley, p. 60.

20. Another tree, the Monterey pine, also grows naturally only on those points, as well as forty-five miles north near Año Nuevo Island, eighty miles south on Santa Rosa Island, and on two islands off Baja California. By the time Weston arrived, both the Monterey cypress and pine had become popular landscaping elements for homesteads, cottages, and mansions throughout Carmel and around the globe. For a fuller discussion of the ecology of these trees, see Gilliam (note 14), pp. 26–28. See also Paul Henson and Donald J. Usner, *The Natural History of Big Sur* (Berkeley, 1993), pp. 209–10 and 217–18. These trees are also discussed in relation to climate and fauna in Joseph Grinnel and Jean M. Linsdale, *Vertebrate Animals of Point Lobos Reserve, 1934–35* (Washington, D.C., 1936), pp. 16–19.

21. Another force that deflects the southbound waters to the west is the Coriolos effect. This results from the rotation of the earth, causing all moving fluids, like wind and water currents, to rotate clockwise in the northern hemisphere and counterclockwise in the southern. See Henson and Usner (note 20), p. 36.

22. Grinnel and Linsdale (note 20), p. 3.

23. The Save-the-Redwoods League had been active since the mid-1920s in helping to save the Monterey cypress. The organization hired the internationally known architectural landscape firm of Frederick Law Olmstead to research Point Lobos. In 1932 Weston entered a print, *Joshua Tree—Mojave Desert* (1928) in the exhibition "California Trees" at the De Young Museum in San Francisco; the Save-the-Redwoods League cosponsored this event with the California Conservation Committee of the Garden Club of America, seeking to publicize the plight of endangered trees. Weston won the first prize of $100; see Amy Conger, *Edward Weston Photographs from the Collection of the Center for Creative Photography* (Tucson, 1992), entry 552.

24. The Allan Memorial Grove, formerly known as Cypress Grove, Monterey Cypress Grove, and Point Lobos Park, is dedicated to the memory of Alexander MacMillan Allan and his wife, Satie Bradley Morgan Allan. They were deserving of the memorial, as they single-handedly saved the peninsula from residential development. In 1898, after the last whaling operations had ceased, Allan purchased most of the land from an unprofitable coal company. One year later, with a Japanese marine biologist, he established a successful abalone cannery along Whaler's Cove (see note 25). Eventually, Allan was able to acquire all the lots that had been sold to individuals for home sites in a development he intended to name Carmelito; it was never realized.

25. Allan's partner in the Point Lobos Canning Company was the Japanese marine biologist Gennosuke Kodani. This was the last commercial use of Point Lobos. During Mexican rule (1822–48) of the California territory, it was a site for grazing cattle. After the California gold rush, Chinese fishermen began living there. In 1855 a stone quarry was established. From 1862 until the late 1880s, Portuguese whalers ran a shore-based operation, employing the highest point (now called Whaler's Knoll) and a signal hill for directing the boats to the position of sighted whales. Most of these activities were confined to the Whaler's Cove area. See Jeff Thomson, *Explore Point Lobos Reserve* (Soquel, Calif., 1997), pp. 7–13.

26. Quoted in Grinnel and Linsdale (note 20), p. 158.

27. Weston (note 9), vol. 2, p. 207.

28. Ibid., p. 261.

29. His studio was in Carmel's Seven Arts Court building.

30. See Weston (note 9), vol. 2, p. 279, for a discussion of Weston's concerns about his portrait business and his decision to make unretouched portraits.

31. In 1932, when Armitage published Weston's first book of photographs (see note 11), it was rare that a photographer was able to realize a publication dedicated exclusively to his or her artistic work.

NOTES

32. Wilson (note 16), p. 60.

33. Weston (note 9), vol. 2, p. 206.

34. From "A Statement by Edward Weston," in Charis Wilson Weston and Edward Weston, *California and the West* (New York, 1940), p. 126.

35. Wilson (note 16), p. 89.

36. Wilson Weston and Weston (note 34), p. 124.

37. Ibid., p. 118.

38. The details of the acquisition of the property and the building of the studio on Wildcat Hill are told in Wilson (note 16), pp. 181–90. On the marriage of Weston and Wilson, see note 47.

39. For a more complete description of Genthe's home and studio, see Genthe (note 15), p. 73.

40. Wilson (note 16), p. 186.

41. In 1937 the road leading from Carmel through the Carmel Highlands to Big Sur was connected to Santa Barbara and named the San Simeon Highway. (Weston's mailing address in the Carmel Highlands still employed the name Coast Road, however.) This allowed tourists access to the central California coast below Big Sur for the first time. The elevation of the property on which the Weston studio was built helped to isolate it from the increased traffic.

42. Quoted in Wilson (note 16), p. 189.

43. Quoted in A. L. Sadler, *Cha-no-yu: The Japanese Tea Ceremony* (Rutland, Vt., 1962), p. 103.

44. Wilson Weston and Weston (note 34), pp. 119–20.

45. Edward Weston to Cole Weston, Dec. 2, 1938, in Paulette Weston, ed., *Laughing Eyes: A Book of Letters between Edward and Cole Weston* (Carmel, Calif., 2000), p. 68.

46. Jeffers, "Shine, Republic" (1935), in Jeffers (note 12), p. 171.

47. Wilson (note 16), p. 206. In an April 15, 1938, letter to Cole, one year before he and Charis were wed, Weston mentioned that San Francisco newspapers had mistakenly reported his marriage. In another note to Cole, written on April 19, 1939, the day he applied for and received a license for marriage, Edward made no mention that he and Charis intended to be married on the anniversary of their first meeting, April 22. Circumstances involving the justice of the peace forced them to postpone the wedding until April 24. The letter in which he mentioned the wedding is dated April 30. See Weston (note 45), p. 59.

48. Edward Weston, "Photographic Art," in *Encyclopedia Britannica*, 14th ed. (New York/Chicago, 1940), vol. 17, pp. 796–99.

49. Wilson (note 16), p. 226. This statement should not imply that Weston gave up his portrait business except for interesting or well-paying sitters. He was a practical man. The revenue from the book although modest was real and probably provided his ego with a psychological boost.

50. Weston (note 9), vol. 2, p. 221.

51. Francis Bacon, "Of Youth and Age," in idem, *The Essays* (Harmondsworth, Eng., 1985), p. 187.

52. The usefulness of the tea-master model for the development of revolutionary ideas is restricted to the arts and humanities. For scientific thought, it is less accurate. For instance in mathematics, which of all fields relies the least on life experience, it is almost totally reversed in its prediction of which decades significant contributions are made. (Blaise Pascal, Isaac Newton, Carl Friedrich Gauss, Evariste Galois, Albert Einstein, and Kurt Gödel all made major contributions to mathematics or mathematical physics before the age of thirty-one.)

53. The photographer Edward Steichen burned most of his early paintings at this point of his career.

54. The photographer Brassaï gave up photography and became a writer before his third period began. Likewise, Henri Cartier-Bresson took up drawing, which he had done in his youth, as his primary medium of expression.

55. Betty Friedan, *The Fountain of Age* (New York, 1993), p. 69.

56. Quoted in Wayne Booth, *The Art of Growing Older: Writers on Living and Aging* (New York, 1992), p. 21.

57. Wallace Stevens, "Puella Parvula" (1950), in *The Collected Poems of Wallace Stevens* (New York, 1990), p. 456.

58. Yamanone Soji-ki, quoted in Louise Allison Cort, "Tea in Japan: From the Late 16th Century to the Present," in Hayshiya Seize, *Chanoyu: Japanese Tea Ceremony* (New York, 1979), p. 25.

59. Robinson Jeffers, "Introduction" to Merle Armitage, ed., *Fifty Photographs: Edward Weston* (New York, 1947); repr. in Beaumont Newhall and Amy Conger, eds. *Edward Weston Omnibus, A Critical Anthology* (Salt Lake City, 1984), p. 92.

60. Adams expressed this sentiment in the memoir he wrote with Mary Street Alinder, *Ansel Adams, An Autobiography* (Boston, 1985), p. 253.

61. In 1591, at the age of seventy, Rikyu was ordered to commit suicide by Toyotomi Hideyoshi, the ruling warrior lord. The reasons vary with different historians.

62. Michelangelo began the *Rondanini Pietà* (Milan, Castello Sforzesco) around 1555, when he was eighty, and left it unfinished. Beethoven wrote his five final quartets in the 1820s; he probably began no. 127 in E flat as early as 1822, when he was fifty-two. He completed the last of the five quartets, no. 135 in F major, during August and September 1826, five months before he died. For a discussion of Beethoven's last quartets as representative of work of the third period of an artist, see Anthony Storr, *Solitude: A Return to the Self* (New York, 1988), pp. 170–73.

63. Wallace Stevens, "The Plain Sense of Things" (1954), in *The Palm at the End of the Mind: Selected Poems and a Play* (New York, 1990), p. 382.

64. Quoted in Beaumont Newhall, *Supreme Instants: The Photography of Edward Weston* (Boston, 1986), p. 39.

65. Robinson Jeffers, "Rearmament" (1935), in Jeffers (note 12), p. 169.

66. Walt Whitman, *Leaves of Grass* (New York, 1942).

67. Weston (note 9), vol. 2, p. 206.

68. Ben Maddow, *Edward Weston: His Life* (Millerton, N.Y., 1979; 2d ed. 1989), p. 268.

69. Alan Trachtenberg, "The Final Years," in Gilles Mora, ed., *Edward Weston: Forms of Passion* (New York, 1995), pp. 289–90.

70. It should be noted that Minor White later commented on the theme of death in Weston's photographs, but was one of the few to do so at the time. See Conger (note 23), p. 40.

71. Charis Wilson observed that the funereal character of Weston's work may be due to over-inked reproductions; see idem, "The Weston Eye," in Peter C. Bunnell and David Featherstone, eds., *EW:100, Centennial Essays in Honor of Edward Weston* (Carmel, Calif., 1986), p. 122.

72. Jeffers's anguish emerges in his 1941 *Be Angry at the Sun* and continues unabated in his 1948 *The Double Axe & Other Poems*, to such an extent that his publisher, Random House, felt obliged to disassociate itself from the poems by stating, in a "publisher's note," "its disagreement over some of the political views pronounced by the poet in this volume."

73. Trachtenberg (note 69), p. 293.

74. Wilson (note 16), p. 297.

75. Ibid., pp. 254–55.

76. Ibid., p. 281.

77. Ibid.

78. When the war focused the Westons' attention on returning home, they decided against the middle route, with its potential for hazardous driving conditions. They were also not prepared to take photographs in frigid weather. Thus, they avoided the big-sky country of the northern Great Plains, as well as the northern Rocky Mountains, where, under more favorable conditions, a wealth of photographic potential might have stimulated Weston the way California did.

79. Weston was no doubt mindful of other photographic visions of the United States that had appeared in books and magazines drawing on the archives of the Farm Security Administration, and on Walker Evans's book *American Photographs* (New York, 1938).

80. Laughlin used Charis as his model for the shroud-covered figure in *Time Phantasm* (fig. 12).

81. Weston to Minor White, [1946], quoted in Conger (note 23), p. 40.

82. Mary Austin, "The Land," from *Stories of the Country of Lost Borders* (1903), quoted in Leonard Michaels et al., eds., *West of the West, Imagining California* (San Francisco, 1989), pp. 107–108. During part of the same period, Walker Evans, a much younger photographer, was also fascinated with cemeteries, wrecked vehicles, dilapidated buildings, and rusting signs. Frederick Sommer photographed in the desert and began producing photographs of dead chickens and their organs. Laura Gilpin also photographed desert landscapes, but not as examples of death or destruction.

83. Wilson (note 16), p. 307.

84. Weston (note 45), p. 98.

85. Quoted in Conger (note 23), p. 39.

86. Ibid.

87. Weston made this photograph around September 1942, not long after Point Lobos was closed to civilians. At this time, he began taking portraits of his immediate family. Charis remembered that he considered the gas mask awful and "hard to make it part of the picture and not the picture." See Conger (note 23), entry 1695.

88. Weston took this photograph around September 1943, when Point Lobos was still closed to civilians. Its title is the same as that of a folksy song, popular at the beginning of the century. See Conger (note 23), entry 1722. About this photograph, Charis wrote:

> I stand on the steps of my workroom eating an apple and holding an "Edward Weston" sign as my brother [Leon, who would serve time as a conscientious objector] looks out the window, playing his recorder. A great deal of our mutual life was commemorated in that picture: the sign was from Edward's Carmel studio; the stone bird with raised wings in one corner was carved by a stone-cutter we met on the Whitman trip; a piled-up rock wall attested to my pleasure in building such walls whenever an earthbank needed holding. Along with such specific mementos, the photograph also contained a general tapestry of Edward's and my territory at Wildcat Hill—blooming geraniums, manzanita, the weathered boards of my workroom, the grey pines on the steep hill behind. Just then Edward was tacking titles on his pictures, and this one was called "My Little Grey Home in the West." The mockery was evident then; now I find it has a poignant ring.

See Charis Wilson, *Nudes* (Millerton, N.Y., 1977), p. 16. A variant of this photograph (Conger [note 23], entry 1695) shows Charis holding a cow's skull.

89. Weston made this photograph around September 1943 at the studio of his friend Jean Kellogg. The models are: Neil (Weston's third son) on the far right, Leon (Charis's brother) in the center window holding an artist's modeling mannequin, Charis in the lower-left window holding a lamp, and Jean Kellogg in the upper-left window. The title refers to a book on visual composition, *The Elements of Dynamic Symmetry* (New York, 1926), by Jay Hambridge, which was popular at the time. See Conger (note 23), entry 1724.

90. Weston took this photograph around July 1943. It is one of four negatives that he saved of what he termed a "very symbolic" series of still lifes. The Dr. Pepper soda package refers to U.S. Senator Claude Pepper, a member of the Foreign Relations Committee whom Weston admired. See Conger (note 23), entry 1721.

91. Wilson (note 16), p. 310.

92. Edward Weston to Brett Weston (and his other sons), June 4, 1943, in Weston (note 45), p. 101: "The artist is invariably an anarchist, while the people, the masses, are inevitably commu-

nists—for reasons of self protection, from sheer fear of walking alone. You will understand I am not speaking of political anarchism or communism. Now as a good anarchist of many years standing I am not the side of the underdog—the little people. . . ."

93. Weston to Minor White, quoted in Conger (note 23), p. 39.

94. Weston wrote to Beaumont and Nancy Newhall after he and Charis had separated: "We began to break down as a team as far back as the Whitman trip. . . ."; quoted in Maddow (note 68), p. 228.

95. Edward Weston, "Statement" in idem, *Fiftieth Anniversary Portfolio 1902–1952*, repr. in Peter C. Bunnell, ed., *Edward Weston on Photography* (Salt Lake City, 1983), p. 151.

96. Quoted in Conger (note 23), p. 39.

97. Edward Weston and Charis Wilson, *The Cats of Wildcat Hill* (New York, 1947).

98. Wilson (note 16), p. 344.

99. Quoted in ibid., pp. 345–46.

100. Robinson Jeffers, "The Old Stonemason," in *Selected Poems* (New York, 1965), p. 92.

101. Amy Conger pointed out that, although this photograph is always dated 1945, the glassine for the negative is dated October 1944; see Conger (note 23), entry 1782.

102. Yeats (note 1), p. 195.

103. Weston to Nancy Newhall, Mar. 3, 1945, quoted in Conger (note 23), entry 1772.

104. Wilson (note 16), pp. 336–37.

105. Quoted in Conger (note 23), p. 41.

106. Ansel Adams, *Letters and Images, 1914–1984* (Boston, 1988), p. 164.

107. Nancy Newhall, *The Photographs of Edward Weston* (New York, 1946).

108. The photographs were donated by Ruth McM. Maitland.

109. See Terence Pitts, *Edward Weston, Color Photography* (Tucson, 1986), pp. 11–12.

110. Minor White, "Lobos 1944–1948, A Selection of Photographs by Edward Weston," *Aperture* 4 (1953), n. pag.

111. Edward Weston, *My Camera on Point Lobos* (Yosemite Park, Calif., 1950).

112. Ansel Adams's book *My Camera in Yosemite Valley* (Boston, 1949) was a commercial success partly because of his photography and partly because Yosemite is much more of a tourist destination than Point Lobos.

113. Dody Thomson, "Edward Weston," *Malahat Review* 14 (Apr. 1970), pp. 39–80; repr. in Newhall and Conger (note 59), pp. 132–51. For Thomson's description of Weston's physical appearance, see p. 135.

114. Ibid., p. 141.

115. Ibid.

116. Ibid.

117. Wallace Stevens, "Credences of Summer" (1947), in idem (note 57), p. 376.

118. Wallace Stevens, "The Poem that Took the Place of a Mountain" (1954), in ibid., p. 512.

119. On October 25, 1979, the United States Board on Geographic Names officially changed the name of Pebbly Beach to Weston Beach after Ansel Adams and Weston's family and friends petitioned to memorialize him at Point Lobos.

Text typeface is Adobe Sabon, based on a 1966 design by Jan Tschichold. The type was chosen for its elegant legibility and the parallel between Tschichold's and Edward Weston's careers. Tschichold was born in 1902 in Leipzig, Germany. In 1925, after having acquired a traditional crafts background, he issued a revolutionary and dogmatic typographic manifesto inspired by the graphic work of El Lissitzky, László Moholy-Nagy, and other artists and craftsmen of the Bauhaus. Published in 1928, his *Die neue Typographie* (The New Typography) widely distributed his ideas. One year later, he designed and coedited with Franz Roh *foto-auge* (photo-eye), which includes the work of Weston, among that of other leading modernist photographers. By 1940 Tschichold had renounced much of the typographic dogma he had championed in his youth and took up more traditional models for type design and imposition. This occurred at the same time that Weston shifted away, although less radically than the designer, from the formalism

COLOPHON

Produced by the Publications Department of The Art Institute of Chicago, Susan F. Rossen, Executive Director

Edited by Susan F. Rossen

Production by Amanda W. Freymann, Associate Director of Publications–Production

Design by Jody Hanson

This book was printed on 100# Aberdeen Silk and bound by Amilcare Pizzi S.p.A. under the supervision of Robert Hennessey, who produced the printing separations and also guided the Art Institute's Alan Newman and Greg Williams in the scanning of the original photographs.

Eleven thousand three hundred copies have been printed to accompany the exhibition *Edward Weston: The Last Years in Carmel*, of which five thousand are for noncommercial use by the Hyatt Vacation Club.

for which he had become famous. Working in his sixties on Sabon, Tschichold returned to his premodernist enthusiasms to study a fourteen-point roman font of 1592 named Saint Augustine and attributed to Claude Garamond. He modeled the italic for Sabon on a font attributed to Robert Granjon that was present on the same specimen sheet as the Saint Augustine. Tschichold designed Sabon to eliminate differences between handset and machine-set texts, and named it after the French punch cutter Jacques Sabon.

The display typeface is Adobe Frutiger, originally designed by Adrian Frutiger in 1976. Frutiger, who was born in Switzerland in 1928 and educated there, worked in France for Deberny & Peignot typefounders, where he developed his best-known typeface, Univers. He designed Frutiger originally for Paris's Charles DeGaulle airport. The University of California Press used a version of this face as the headline display face for its 1995 translation and facsimile of Tschichold's *The New Typography*, since it is the closest approximation in digital form of the original. (D. T.)